The Rescued Soul

The Rescued Soul

Christina Enevoldsen

overcoming sexual abuse
embracing a new life

Overcoming Sexual Abuse
  Scottsdale, Arizona
  Christina@OvercomingSexualAbuse.com

The Rescued Soul,
  a Writing Journey for the Healing of Incest and Family Betrayal
Christina Enevoldsen

First Edition
ISBN 13: 978-0692342916
ISBN 10: 0692342915

Printed in the United States of America

Cover design by Bethany Ruck

Note of Caution

Healing from abuse is very painful. If you feel overwhelmed, please slow down or stop and ask for help from a therapist. It's particularly important to have a therapist's support if you have:

- Suicidal thoughts
- Self-harming behaviors
- Dissociative Identity Disorder
- Difficulty distinguishing between memory and reality or between fantasy and reality

Table of Contents

Introduction

"In every block of marble I see a statue as plain as though it stood before me, shaped and perfect in attitude and action. I have only to hew away the rough walls that imprison the lovely apparition to reveal it to the other eyes as mine see it." —Michelangelo

It's completely fascinating to me to consider how Michelangelo created. The sculptor imagined the finished work before he lifted the chisel to the stone. He didn't see the marble block; he saw the image underneath. He recognized what it was and then simply removed what it was not.

I'm no Michelangelo, but I am creating a masterpiece—or rather, revealing one. My childhood sexual abuse encased me in a false identity and covered me in a shroud of lies. My false self wasn't stone, but it imprisoned me just the same. My healing process has been the chiseling away at the falsehoods to free my true self.

The trouble was that I didn't begin with the clarity of Michelangelo. The only Christina I'd ever known was the one who adapted to the abuse. The lies entrapped me for so long that I felt I didn't exist apart from them. How could I have a vision for someone I've never seen? That was my question when I began my healing. I didn't know the answer but I was determined to rescue my true image just as the great artist rescued his beauties from the stone.

As I discovered, I didn't need to see or *make* myself into anything. I am who I am. I was so used to contorting myself into certain roles that I thought I would achieve the real me the same way. In reality, all I needed to do was remove the lies. As I've healed, the real me has emerged without even thinking about it. It's natural and unrehearsed. I was there all along.

I'm convinced that the most debilitating and devastating effect of abuse is the loss of self. The disconnection from the true self leaves survivors absolutely abandoned. This leads to a lifetime of utter loneliness and isolation. To attempt to cover the loss, survivors seek out unhealthy dependence on relationships, chemicals, work, thrills—anything to outrun the awareness of the void. It's this disconnection that leads to all the other effects of abuse that survivors are familiar with.

1

But there is vitaly fulfilling life after abuse.

Writing has been the key to rescuing myself from my ostracized existence. Through my writing, I've repaired my relationship with myself and the world I interact with. I write as a means to sort through the confusion of the lies so I can see the truth. I gain clarity about my experiences, thoughts and feelings. I know myself better by getting more in touch with my past and how it shaped me.

Even though I've used this writing tool for years, I'm still amazed every time I use it. I know there's no magic solution to this healing process, but the power in writing seems magical to me. It's as though the pen has some secret wisdom and I have only to access it. In reality, I know the wisdom and solutions come from within me and that my hands, mind and heart are working together to bring it forth.

Preparing for Your Journey

I invite you to start your own writing journey. Each chapter in this book begins with my personal process of taking another step in the healing journey. It concludes with suggestions for you to take your own steps. I've also included one of the most powerful tools I've used in my healing, which is a memories journal. At the end of the book, I've provided a second journal space with enough writing prompts to last a year if you do one a day.

As you read, try to stay emotionally engaged. Feel your feelings; stay present in your body and pay attention to what's going on inside of you. If you get to the end of a page and recognize that you don't remember what you just read, stop. What did you read or think about that felt threatening? What did you feel? What did it remind you of? What was so threatening about it? Take the time to comfort yourself before you continue.

As you write, listen to the voice in your head responding to what you're writing. Do you feel threatened or afraid of recording your thoughts? Is the voice you hear harsh? Does it criticize? Do you believe what you say? Do you believe your thoughts and feelings are important?

If you don't value your feelings and thoughts or if you're afraid to express them, who taught you to feel that way? Does that voice remind you of anyone in particular? Who spoke to you that way?

As you listen to your inner voice, challenge the judgments. Making judgments about yourself is a dysfunctional way to protect yourself. What are those judgments trying to protect you from? Are they meant to shame you into silence to avoid rejection or abandonment? Do you think you deserve to be discounted if you don't think, believe, feel or act a particular way? Do you believe you need to express yourself perfectly to be acknowledged? Even by yourself?

Introduction

Judgment causes separation, which leads to feeling more abandoned. Even if you don't like what you write, try to read it with curiosity rather than judgment. Use it to build intimacy with yourself. Pay attention to what's in your heart and use it as a way to lovingly say to yourself, "Your concerns, feelings and well-being have been ignored for long enough and I'm not going to do that to you anymore."

Abuse meant secrets and lies. Survival meant silence. Writing down your feelings and thoughts is a wonderful way to break your silence and to tell your truth.

This is your book and it's up to you how you want to use it. If you just read along instead of doing any writing, that's okay. If you skip around and only read or write what you feel like, that's okay. Take breaks and go as slowly as you choose. You're not compromising anything in the quality of your recovery to be gentle with yourself. Sometimes, your pain, memories or circumstances will dictate what you work on first. The important thing is to move forward in your own timing.

Since healing is cyclical, this book can be used repeatedly. Every time you go back over it, you'll be prepared for more depth and you'll understand things in a different light. It may bring up truth that you weren't ready to face before or it might show you how far you've come.

In the early stages of healing, the mess you have going on inside you seems overwhelming. It's common to want to frantically stuff it all back inside the best you can and try to cover it up. If you commit to the process, face your fear, sort out the lies, and embrace the truth, you'll come out the other side feeling like a whole person. You'll have more energy to really live instead of spending it running for your life. You are worth everything you invest in your restoration.

Of course, the steps I've taken can't be neatly passed on to you. This book is intended to give you hope, inspiration, encouragement and insights, but we each have a unique path to healing and it's up to you to create your own path. Only you can heal you. That thought may seem overwhelming, but in small steps, it's much easier. And you don't really have to be alone on this journey. I can't heal *for* you, but I can heal *with* you. We'll share the journey together. You're not alone.

If you think you'd benefit from the support of other survivors on your healing journey or are looking for a deeper level of engagement, I invite you to participate in our group coaching program, using this book as our guide. For more information, visit: **http://overcomingsexualabuse.com/group-coaching-program/**

The Rescued Soul

1
Separated, Isolated, Abandoned

When I was nine years old, my father orally raped me in the corner of the airplane hangar that was behind our house. The act forced on me was confusing, disgusting and frightening. I was alone with my father, but his glassy-eyed expression made me feel like he was a million miles away.

That was one incident of sexual abuse among countless acts that my father perpetrated on me over the course of years. My dad traded me to other men—privately and in groups. Some instances were planned, while others seemed opportunistic. I was never safe.

I witnessed the abuse from above my body. Being connected to my body was intolerable. Allowing my mind to escape by viewing the scenes from above gave me some relief from the emotional and physical pain of the abuse. My body couldn't escape, but my mind could.

Abuse was a way of life and so was dissociation. I lived separated from myself, never feeling like my body was a safe place to be.

The separateness that protected me from harmful touch also isolated me from *any* touch. I couldn't sense connection with anyone. I was driven to be with others—not being with someone else made me feel like I didn't exist—but whatever the relationship, I always felt alone. It was as though I lived in a bubble.

My father's abuse penetrated more than just my body. My very being was contaminated by the false identity it forced on me. My dad's actions were an accusation. Through the abuse, he communicated to me that I didn't have the value of other children. I wasn't worthy of protection. I wasn't worthy of real love. I wasn't a real person; I was an object, only useful for disgusting things and then discarded. I was trash.

The abuse invalidated my opinions, desires, thoughts, feelings, and my very life. The violation told me that I didn't matter. My cries of pain didn't deter him; my desire to get away didn't stop him.

My mother reinforced my feelings and beliefs about myself. To her, I was invisible. I felt as though I couldn't do anything to make her see me. I was unworthy of attention or comfort or love or acceptance. I didn't belong anywhere.

I wasn't aware that it was the abuse that taught me those things about myself. I thought I was abused because those things were true. I thought I was inherently worthless so I deserved whatever anyone did to me. I wasn't old enough or secure enough in my own self-identity so I was defenseless against the lies.

Throughout my life, I reacted to those lies by trying to prove they weren't true. I knew they were actaully true—they were the only truth I'd known—but I was desperate to escape from them. I wore masks to hide from the awful person I thought I was. I played roles out of some hope of being accepted. I studied people to figure out what they wanted. I conformed. My whole life felt like a performance.

One of my false selves was the "hard worker." I projected an image of responsibility, maturity, and dependability. It was my uniform that showed people I was useful. On other occasions, I was the seductress, the mentor, the tough girl, or the cheerful girl.

I thought wearing masks would make me more likeable, but I eliminated the possibility for deep relationships by constructing a barrier. Looking back, I can see why I experienced so much rejection. People couldn't relate to my false front. Even if someone did connect with that false persona, it wasn't the type of connection I longed for since it was based on a lie.

I could never have real intimacy. I rejected my true self before I even gave people the chance to accept or reject me. The rejection of my true self led to putting on a false self, which led to rejection by others, which led to more rejection from me. What a very vicious cycle that was!

Cumulative Effects

Every aspect of my abuse was a disconnection from my identity and individuality. It was a denial and dismissal of my value and physical, emotional, spiritual, and mental boundaries.

The abuse separated me from my personhood. I was an object to be used for someone else's enjoyment. My wants and needs weren't considered. My welfare was dismissed. I didn't have permission to say no or to run away.

My defense was to separate from my mind, emotions and body. I mentally pushed the abuse away:

- Out of body experience/watching from the ceiling.
- Finding a focal point in the room and shutting off everything else.
- Imagining being somewhere else.
- Telling myself, "This isn't happening" or "It's just a dream" or "I'm imagining things."

- "He loves me. This is a normal way to show affection."
- "I deserve this."
- "I asked for this."
- "He's just teaching me about sex for my own good."

The lies that I told myself further separated me from myself and from reality.

More lies were invented to protect the secret. I needed to pretend that everything was fine. I was happy.

The secret kept me isolated. I needed to keep my distance to keep the secret. Guarding my actions, guarding my words. My family and the rest of the world went on as usual while I was shattered.

I remained an outsider in my own life. I dissociated when I felt threatened or overwhelmed. Without a healthy foundation, that was most of the time. I turned to addictions to avoid feeling and knowing. Being me—whoever that was—was too painful.

Rescuing Myself

Rescuing myself from the isolation meant untangling the messy net of lies. Lie by lie, I freed myself. Despite all the ways I'd disconnected from myself, I'm a whole person now. I'm delighted with me. I'm good, fulfilling company for myself. I'm a solid presence in my own life. I can connect with others now since I'm connected to myself. I have deeply fulfilling relationships based on truth—who I really am—a unique and lovable person.

Suggested writing:

Do you see evidence in your own life of the separation from your true identity?

What are some ways you can relate to the isolation?

Can you think of ways the disconnection kept you isolated from other relationships?

What are some life choices you made to protect your false identity?

2
Returning to My Own Side: Dealing With Shame

I was twenty-two. I'd been married five years when I confessed to my husband that I'd been having an affair with someone in his family. My husband needed some time away from me to consider what he wanted to do so he arranged for me to stay with my parents.

When I arrived at my parents' house, I sat in one corner of their living room while my mom and dad sat in the opposite corner. The living room was mostly used as a pass through to get from the front door to the rest of the house. But on this day, I wasn't allowed entrance to the rest of the house quite yet. The entrance fee was hearing their disapproval. Their shaming message was, "How could you turn out so bad when you came from such a good family?"

I desperately wanted my parents to tell me that they loved me despite my recent behavior. I knew I didn't deserve it, but I ached for it.

At the time, I didn't consider the injustice of my dad's judgment. He'd given me to other men when I was a little girl. If it was wrong for me to pass myself around, then why wasn't it wrong for him? While I sat there with them, that never occurred to me. I was just grateful that they had given me shelter. I didn't expect anything more.

Throughout my healing process, I thought of that incident again and again. I never seemed to get past it. I finally had some insights about it while I was reading a story from another abuse survivor. She had coped with her pain through a dangerous addiction. Her experience was horrific, but the way she wrote about it felt detached and distant. She seemed to be writing about someone she didn't know well or didn't care about instead of telling the story of her own life.

I read and reread her story, curious to know its significance for me. I finally asked myself if there was anything in my past that I was disconnected from. Immediately, I saw myself back in my parents' living room.

As my mom and dad situated themselves far from me, I was sitting with them. My inward posture toward myself was just as rejecting, just as judging, just as shaming as theirs. They didn't want to associate with me, they didn't want to touch me, but I didn't want to touch me either. I was saying to myself, "If I could get away from you, I would."

9

Looking at the Origins

When my dad orally raped me in the hangar behind our house, it faced a public road that was only separated by a large field of tumbleweed and tall, dead grass. I was panicked—but not because of the act being perpetrated on me—I was terrified of being caught. In my mind, I was the bad one. When he was finished, my dad threw my head off him in disgust. His sudden thrust seemed to demand, "How could you???" as though he were the victim of the rape.

That incident reinforced what I knew about myself: I was disgusting. I believed my badness meant that I had to forfeit love. I thought others fleeing from me was justified. In my shame, I abandoned myself.

I felt shame from having the affair, but my shame didn't originate from the affair. Rather, the affair was the result of my shame. I accepted the shame as my identity and behaved accordingly. I treated myself the way I was treated in that airplane hangar, in my parents' bedroom, in my own bed, at the sex parties and everywhere else my dad violated me.

I was treated like trash so I believed I was trash, but that didn't make me trash. I was misused. I was mishandled. It wasn't something I deserved and it wasn't me.

I was punishing myself through my affair as a way of expressing my shame. Hating myself kept me in the cycle of self-abuse. Judging myself kept me disconnected in a way that didn't allow me any power to change. I needed to forgive myself for the ways I adapted to the abuse. I had more compassion for myself when I considered the reasons for my behavior:

• I never had permission to say no.
• I thought my value was through sex.
• I thought sex with family members was okay as long as it was a secret.
• I sought out comfort through sex since the only touch I received as a child was sexual touch.

My affair was also a way to express the fear and pain of my childhood abuse. It echoed the same emotions that were unexpressed and unresolved:

• Powerless (through the compulsion)
• Demeaning
• Secrecy (and the fear of being caught)
• Rejection

Taking a more objective look at the roots of my behavior allowed me to be more understanding of myself. Today, I can separate the wrong things I've done

Returning to My Own Side: Dealing With Shame

from the wrong things that have been done to me. I don't condone or defend the ways I've hurt others or myself, but I don't abandon myself either. I can acknowledge harmful behavior while still being my own ally. I'm loyal to myself the same way I stand with my children when they fail.

Over the years, I've done some things that have led to other people separating from me. No matter what I've done in my past or what I'll do in the future, I don't separate from myself anymore. I sit with myself during the tough times with my arms wrapped around me saying, "I'm not going anywhere."

Suggested writing:

What are some of the ways you coped with your abuse? Drug or alcohol abuse? Compulsive gambling? Excessive care-taking? Cutting or other type of self-harm? Hoarding? Compulsive eating? Compulsive sex?

In what ways do the coping methods give you comfort?

In what ways do the coping methods echo the same feelings or dynamics of your abuse?

What are some reasons that you coped in those ways? What beliefs about yourself led you to those behaviors?

Returning to My Own Side: Dealing With Shame

Can you show yourself some understanding and compassion for using those coping methods? Can you forgive yourself?

Finish this sentence:

I can forgive myself for the destructive ways I coped because…

Or:

I can't forgive myself for the destructive ways I coped because…

Does the reason you gave for not being willing to forgive yourself give you any insights about what beliefs you still have about yourself that might be lies?

The Rescued Soul

3
Focused on Me

Several years ago, I had a friend whose husband wasn't treating her right. Some days, my friend had enough and prepared herself for a life without him. Other days, she wanted to give him another chance. She spent months wavering between leaving and staying.

I knew better than to try to give any advice. My role as her friend was to listen to her and to cry with her. I could share from my experience, but I couldn't tell her what to do. Still, I struggled to stay on the sidelines.

Having escaped from an abusive twenty-one year marriage years earlier, I knew that it was hard to leave. My friends had told me the same things I was itching to tell my friend—he didn't deserve another chance; I could do better. But I was the one who would have to live with my choices so it had to be my decision.

I knew that about my friend's situation. I knew that leaving her abusive husband would only be the right choice for her if she were the one making it.

In spite of knowing that, I could barely hold myself back from shouting, "Leave that *#*@*!" It was as though I was in a life or death struggle. There was such force in my urge to tell her what to do that there had to be something unhealthy behind it.

I realized that I wasn't trying to help my friend; I was trying to help the me from my past. I wanted to scream to my younger self, "Get away from that man! He's no good for you. Every minute you stay, he drains more life from you!"

There wasn't anything I could do to change that. I stayed with my ex-husband far too long, but I left as soon as I felt ready. My friend's situation didn't have anything to do with my own. Even if I could convince her to leave her husband, that wouldn't change the fact that I had stayed with mine. My past wouldn't be undone by "helping" someone else. I had to deal with the pain and grief within my own heart; resolution couldn't be found in someone else's life.

That's a lesson that I've had to come back to again and again. One of the biggest challenges of my life, and especially my healing process, has been to remain focused on me.

Changing My Focus

In my early days of working with survivors of sexual abuse, I was chatting with a friend and fellow advocate. With her children still at home, she expressed how careful she needed to be in the time she lent to her work. Both of us agreed how challenging it was to find balance in caring for our families and working in a field that we're so passionate about.

I was silently celebrating in my mind, "My kids are adults now. I'm free to serve as much as I want!"

A meek little voice interrupted my thoughts. "I'm still here," she pleaded. In an instant, I understood that I still had *me* to care for. I felt a bit of tenderness for myself, but it was overshadowed by annoyance. Grudgingly, I made a list of things I should do to take better care of myself and started to work through them.

As I started, I heard the impatience in my thoughts as though I was waiting outside of myself, tapping my foot, rushing myself through whatever I was doing. I caught myself demanding, "More important people are waiting for you. Hurry up!"

Even when I did pleasant things for myself, it was a chore to complete. The things that most people enjoyed were a burden to me—I was a burden.

That was a familiar feeling. It was the same attitude my mother had about children, about *me*. She took care of my physical needs, but she seemed to resent how exhausting I was.

Just as my mother never found joy in caring for me, I never did either. It saddened me that I didn't find pleasure in doing nice things for myself. I grieved for how my mother treated me and for how I'd learned to treat myself.

Validating My Needs

When I was two or three years old, my parents were caring for my infant brother and I needed something. Impatiently, they dismissed me, "Do you think you're the only one who matters? You need to be a big girl and stop whining." That was one of many times my parents communicated to me that I wasn't important; my needs didn't matter; I was selfish to ask for them.

Whenever I had needs, I felt the same shame and abandonment. Since I didn't matter, I had to do something so I wouldn't be abandoned. I needed to work and perform for my value since I was worthless in myself.

I was so used to having my feelings and needs discounted that I learned to do the same thing. I served and gave at my expense. I took care of others while neglecting myself.

Most of the time I really didn't mind helping people. There was a certain high that went with it. I felt powerful—like a superhero. I didn't feel empowered or entitled to help myself, but it felt good to serve others. It was like a drug. Easing the pain of a friend helped me to avoid my own pain. But my pain always came back and I needed to serve and serve and serve so I could keep feeling better. I thought I was so loving, but I was really just coping. I wasn't even loving myself.

I sometimes wondered when it would be my turn to have my needs met. So many false beliefs prevented me from nurturing myself:

- I believed other people were more important than me.
- I felt ashamed for having needs. I believed it was selfish to take care of my own needs.
- In my shame, I couldn't ask directly for my needs to be met. I hoped that if I were compliant enough or helpful enough, eventually someone would notice my needs and meet them.
- I thought it was my duty to take care of everyone else's emotional, sexual and physical needs.
- I didn't feel I had value simply for existing; I had to earn my space on earth by serving others.
- Taking care of others was a way for me to feel more power. I didn't feel empowered to take care of me, but I felt powerful by helping others.
- Investing so much of my time and energy into other people's lives distracted me from the pain and discontent of my life.

The truth is that my value doesn't come from anyone else and it does not go up or down based on what I do. I am valuable because I exist. My needs are important because I'm important and I'm empowered to fulfill them.

Identifying My Needs

In the beginning of my healing, I had a tough time recognizing my needs. It was hard to distinguish between being hungry, sleepy, sad, angry, or achy. I was so used to ignoring my feelings and needs that I dismissed the signals. I was much more aware of other people's feelings and needs than I was of my own.

I wrote a letter to myself to try to reconcile:

Dear Self,

I feel like I don't even know you. You seem completely foreign to me. I don't know what you want or what you need. If you want me to take better care of you, you'll have to speak up because I'm busy and I don't have time to stand around trying to break your code or figure you out. Oh! I just realized that you getting "louder" might mean getting my attention in other ways like my body breaking down. I don't want that! I guess I need to learn to listen to you better. Shit!

Honestly, I know I need to, but it seems like a lot of trouble.

Not only that, if I really listen to what you need, what else will I hear? You seem like a big ball of pain. Pain and trouble. If I really took care of you, what would that mean? You seem consuming—like an endless cavern of needs. I want a life—a life apart from YOU!!!

I'm SO frustrated! The abuse messed me up so bad. I just want to be normal and healthy and not have to work so hard at trying to take care of you. Shouldn't I want to do nice things for you? Shouldn't I care that you're not doing very well? I hate that my motivation for trying to take better care of you is that I'm afraid of ending up with some kind of illness.

You deserve better. I believe that even though I don't feel that right now. I wish you had someone better than me to take care of you, but you're stuck with me.

I feel inadequate. I feel like a toddler trying to carry a big person. I'm not enough. I'm struggling just to make it through each day. I feel like taking care of you is too overwhelming. Just thinking about it makes me feel like I can't get enough air—like I'm suffocating or drowning.

It was illuminating to see how inadequate I felt to take care of myself. Feeling powerless has prevented me from making important changes in my life. I was reminded of my abusive first marriage. I had the power to leave all along, but believing I was powerless kept me there. I had to consider that I was empowered to care for my needs even if I didn't feel that way.

I also wrote a letter *from* myself:

Dear Christina,

I know you've heard so many bad things about me but they aren't true. Please don't leave me. I need you. I need you to listen to me. You've been so busy with everyone else and everything else but I'm important too!

I know that you feel overwhelmed trying to care for me, but you wouldn't feel that way if you actually DID take care of me. You wouldn't feel so weak or pulled apart. You think I'm a burden, but I'm not a burden. I'm the answer to feeling so much better about your life. If you made me a priority instead of exhausting yourself with everyone else's needs, you'd actually have more energy. You'd have a real life instead of whatever it is you've been doing. I'm not the problem you've accused me of being! I'm your solution!

I need to you to rest more. I need you to give me more sleep. I need you to feed me healthy food. You know I'm going to get hungry and that I need to eat throughout the day so start planning for that instead of acting like it's a big surprise and inconvenience.

I also need a lot more time without noise or activity. You drown out my voice when you always have something going on. That's something that makes me mad. You blame me for not giving you better signals for what I need, but you intentionally ignore me by filling every waking moment. You'll hear me if you sit still and be quiet.

I was surprised by what I wrote. I expected a whiny plea. I started writing that way, but then it became very strong and direct. The power was unexpected. Maybe I had more strength than I gave myself credit for.

I was also surprised by the truth it revealed about the benefit of taking good care of myself. As I've seen in the years since then, taking care of myself first has empowered me to truly live an empowered life that I love.

Gradually, I've learned to reconnect the signals I'd ignored. As I've honored my needs by attending to them, it's become easier to hear them. I frequently check in with myself throughout each day to hear my thoughts and feelings. I plan my schedule to allow for breaks when I sit still in silence. When I'm driving, I rarely turn on the radio. I stay present, allowing time to think and to hear.

My life is completely different now. I used to fit in time for myself between everything else (if at all) and now I fit in everything else after I've taken care of me. I used to hope that someone else would take care of me—that all my hard work would be recognized and someone would designate my turn. I realized that *is* my turn.

Suggested writing:

Finish these sentences:
   When I think about making myself my priority, I feel…

   My needs are important because…

The Rescued Soul

What are the things that keep you from nurturing yourself?

Where did you get the idea that your needs aren't important?

How would your life be different if you took care of yourself first?

Focused on Me

Write a letter to yourself. Share how you feel about nurturing yourself. No matter what feelings come out, try to conclude with how you plan to start taking better care of yourself. If you can't commit to better self-care, that's okay. Go on to the next letter and see if you can come up with a plan afterwards.

The Rescued Soul

Write a letter *from* yourself. Express how you feel about your needs being ignored. Ask for your needs to be heard and made a priority. Note specific needs that you have.

4

Being Here for Myself: Coping vs. Connecting

I don't remember my mother ever cuddling with me. She wasn't affection-
ate or comfortable with emotions. Her way of dealing with my pain was to feed
me. Especially chocolate. When I ate chocolate, I stopped crying. I shut up and
stopped bothering her.

Chocolate was my solace, but it had some painful effects. When I started
to gain weight in my teen years, my dad restricted my eating. Fat was disgusting to him. Rather than being glad that he didn't like my growing body, I felt
crushed. I comforted myself with one of the only ways I knew, which was
more eating.

I felt shameful to eat and shameful to be fat. I had to hide my chocolate
consumption so I sneaked around as though I were having a secret love affair. I
planned rendezvous with my love. The secrecy added to the excitement, but also
to my sense of isolation.

I turned to chocolate throughout my life, but never more than when my
memories of sexual abuse surfaced. I binged on hazelnut candy bars, chocolate
chip cookies and rocky road ice cream. There was a little voice inside my head
telling me I had already suffered enough and I deserved a little cake or a few
truffles. I was entitled to be nice to myself.

But how much dessert would it take to make up for the sexual abuse?
How many cookies would equal the amount of love I never got? I could
buy out every bakery in the world and still feel the loss. My pain wasn't
caused by being deprived of chocolate so mountains of chocolate couldn't
remove it.

I was doing to myself what my mom had done to me when she gave me
chocolate to stop my crying. By turning to chocolate when I was in pain, I was
saying to myself, "Get away from me and shut up!"

Covering the Pain of Abandonment

As a child, it was intolerable to be left alone with my pain. No one held
me or told me that pain was normal and not something to fear. Pain meant my
mom would push me away.

Abandonment was a death sentence. It said, "You're not worthy of protection, security, comfort or shelter." Masking the pain was survival. It was the very best I could do.

As an adult, I still believed that pain—and the abandonment that followed—led to death.

Figuring out where my addiction was coming from wasn't enough. Only thinking through the problem kept me emotionally distant from myself the same way my mom had been.

I needed to provide what was lacking in my childhood—I had to validate my hurt and comfort my pain. When I felt insecure, I needed assurance; when I felt sad, I needed comfort; when I was mad, I needed understanding. I thought I deserved chocolate, but I really deserved love and nurturing. I learned to give myself the compassionate attention that I really craved.

What Does "Being Nice to Myself" Really Mean?

I justified my compulsive eating by telling myself I was being nice to myself until I discovered that it wasn't as nice as I thought. Then I began defining "nice" differently: It meant staying present in my pain. I thought that meant feeling *all* the pain, *all* the time.

Then I discovered that I needed to adjust my definition of "being nice" to myself again.

Learning what self-love is, I've become more gentle with myself by providing more breaks from the healing process. I found that my biggest breakthroughs come after I take a break. Numbing myself gives me a reprieve from the intensity of healing or other life issues so I can rest.

Coping as a lifestyle communicated to me, "I can't deal with you! You're too needy!" But using healthy coping methods in a nurturing way can communicate, "I notice how tired you are. Come rest for a little while."

Using my coping methods for my benefit requires me to ask, "Am I doing what's best for me now?" I need to decide that from the perspective of an empowered adult instead of a panicked child. That means knowing when to push forward to face the pain and when to back off until another time.

My Gentle Rescue

This morning, I watched the movie, *You've Got Mail*. I've seen it a hundred times. It's my go-to movie when I'm sick. It takes my mind off my pain enough so I can get some sleep. I also watch it when I'm not feeling emotionally well.

With my book release date already announced and much more writing to do, I wasn't supposed to watch a movie. I've struggled writing this chapter more than any other. It's one of my last to complete. I can easily write about painful events from my past and the embarrassing ways the abuse has affected my life, but writing about how I use my coping methods feels threatening. I feel like by defining how I use them, they are being taken away.

After so much loss, that feels like too much. I'm a child again and I'm lost without them. I have a vision of myself in the middle of the ocean, clinging to drifting debris. Then, my only hope for survival is ripped away from me.

That wasn't the time to push myself. I gave myself a break and watched my movie. No harsh reprimands, no guilt trip. I gave myself the time off.

While I was still insisting to myself that I follow my schedule, the panic created internal chaos and so I didn't know why I was feeling lost or what to do about it. Being gentle with myself encouraged much easier internal dialogue.

After comforting myself, I saw what triggered me. While I was writing about my relationship with chocolate, it felt like my dad had caught me again and would take it away.

I don't remember the last time I even ate chocolate. I used to keep a big stash of it, but I don't care about it anymore. I don't need it. I don't like pain, but I can tolerate pain now. I don't associate it with abandonment anymore.

The child within me didn't know any of that. She was still suffering alone, feeling deprived of her only friend in the world. She was left to face the criticisms about her body and the other abuses without any buffer. It was too much for her.

But it's not too much for me. And I'm here for her now. This is how I calmed her down:

> *"What you went through was horrible. I hate how your mom cast aside you and your pain. You deserved so much better than what she gave you. You had to learn to make do with chocolate since that's all you were offered. Then your dad not only took that away from you, but he berated you for chocolate's effect on your body. I feel your desperation, rejection and isolation. I admire you so much for having the ability to keep going with so few resources.*
>
> *"I know that you're terrified that the one thing you had left, the only thing you could rely on, is being taken away. I'm not going to trivialize your terror by telling you that you don't need that. It makes complete sense to me why you cling to it so strongly. It was vital to your survival and I'm so thankful that you survived.*
>
> *"I know you think that chocolate is still all you have, but that's not true anymore. You have me now. I won't cast you aside. I'm crying with you. Cry all you need. Let me hold you and rock you. I won't leave."*

My inner child reacts out of her pain and fear and struggle. As an adult, I'm much better equipped to decide the best action to take. I need to rescue her from her abuse-filled world, but before she's willing to come with me, I have to be willing to go to her. I have to sit with her and identify with her experience and emotions. I have to respect her viewpoint and offer her understanding and compassion. That's the only way she'll trust me enough to let me rescue her.

Since I've been facing my emotions regularly for several years, I don't have the storm of emotions that I used to have so it doesn't take long to process them and move on. With my inner child at peace again, I'm back at writing, feeling good. The funny thing is, once I started feeling "found" again, I realized that I'd been singing a song to myself all morning, even before I realized that I felt lost. The song was, "Bridge Over Troubled Water". I was trying to soothe myself all along.

There's no doubt that comfort is important, even as an adult. Comfort was the best I could do when I was a child, but I'm not a child anymore. Now that I'm pursuing my well-being over comfort, I have emotional health *and* comfort.

Suggested writing:

How did you deal with your pain when you were a child?

How do you deal with it now?

Being Here for Myself: Coping vs. Connecting

When you think about sitting with your feelings, what do you feel?

If you resist sitting with your pain, where is your fear coming from?

In what ways are you "present" for yourself when you're hurt or afraid?

If you usually numb yourself when you're in pain, what are the real needs you have?

How can you find ways to give yourself what you really need?

What are some ways you can determine how to use your coping methods to help you instead of hurt you? What are some questions you can ask yourself to determine if you are deciding as an empowered adult or a panicked child?

5
Making a Home for Myself: Adopting My Inner Child

A little girl used to show up at my doorstep fairly often. She had a knack for arriving at the most inconvenient times and was always so needy. For such a little girl, she had some big problems. I knew that much without even opening the door.

I wasn't going to let her problems become my problems. When I heard her little pathetic cry, I busied myself in projects to take my mind off her or I turned up the volume on the television so I couldn't hear her scratches on the door. I wanted to scream, "GO FUCK SOMEBODY SO THEY'LL TAKE CARE OF YOU!!!!" I was deperate for her to leave me alone.

No matter how much I ignored her, she wouldn't go away. I was exhasted trying to drown out her pleas for help, so begrudgingly, I let her in.

She'd always seemed so determined, but suddenly, she seemed unsure whether it was safe to enter. She made a few hestitating steps toward me and stopped. As a warning that my patience was being drained, I moved the door a few inches toward her. Aware of my meaning, she passed through the doorway, glanced up at me and then her eyes returned to the ground.

It was my first time taking a good look at her. Astonished by the wounds that covered her body, I whispered, "What did they do to you?" Instinctively, I reached out to her, but she winced.

We faced each other in silence, both of us waiting for me to offer something— anything that might help. I just didn't know what to say or do. After some time, I finally told her in a not-so-gentle tone, "I think you need a bath."

She didn't object. In fact, she seemed willing to put herself completely in my care. It saddened me that she consented to trust me after I'd treated her so badly and offered her so little hope for kindness.

While I was bathing her, I examined her. It felt uncomfortably intimate even to touch her arms, but I willed my eyes and heart to see the places she'd been violated. Her body told her story. In that moment, I committed to making a home for her.

I'd heard of inner child exercises for years in relation to inner healing, but it never appealed to me. I reasoned that it was too ethereal or "out there" for me. In truth, I resisted it because I instinctively knew how painful it would be to connect with myself on such an intimate level. I'd been protecting myself from that kind of pain all my life.

I don't remember what finally convinced me to try "meeting" my child within. It may have been all the testimonies from other survivors who claimed it was beneficial. Whatever it was, my first time didn't go very well.

I imagined meeting my nine year old inner child in the front yard of our house. I wanted to meet her outside the house because I was afraid of encountering one or both of my parents inside.

I saw her sitting in the grass with her head resting on her folded knees. Her hands covered her head. I approached her, intending to offer her love and acceptance, but I felt the urge to get away from her and to tell her that she was repulsive and too ugly to be loved.

I'd never heard of anyone being abusive in an inner child encounter and it scared me. I was horrified that I could be so cruel. It was shocking to feel the intensity of my self-hate. Afraid of doing more damage to myself, I backed off for a few weeks before I tried again.

The next time, I imagined myself inside my childhood home. It was bedtime and I sat on my inner child's bed to tuck her in. Expecting to hug and kiss her, instead, I surprised her and me by leaning on her arm to break it. It pleased me to pretend to be nice but to abuse her instead.

In my mind, it was her fault that I was abused. It was her smallness and weakness and vulnerability that caused it.

I wrote her a letter:

Dear Little Christina,

I've been blaming you for "getting yourself" abused. You were small, but that's not a crime. There's nothing wrong about being small. It doesn't justify the things they did to you. Being bigger isn't a license to do harm.

I've also judged you for being weak. You actually were weak in the sense that you were powerless to stop the things that happened to you, but that doesn't make you at fault. In another sense, you were (and are) incredibly strong. You survived so much violation and degradation, but you remain such a compassionate and caring person. That makes you very strong. I'm amazed by that quality in you.

I've hated you for being vulnerable. Vulnerability feels like an invitation to abuse. It feels like a banner that announces, "Come and get me!" But when I think of it the other way, I don't pounce on other people just because I can. I don't go around looking for people smaller or weaker than me so I can attack them. When I find someone's vulnerability, my impulse is to protect and cover them, not to use it against them.

Making a Home for Myself: Adopting My Inner Child

I think I'm seeing that the problem was never you in the first place. You didn't cause the abuse. I'm so sorry for turning against you and unjustly accusing you. I know how painful that is. My parents have done the same to me.

I want to have a closer relationship with you, but I'm afraid. I feel inadequate for you to depend on me. I didn't have anyone to take care of me in the ways that you need so I don't know how to take care of you.

I feel like you're better off without me. I struggle just to care for myself so I'm not too hopeful that I'll be able to care for you. They say that animals and children sense untrustworthy people and I'm scared that you'll know that I'm a bad person. Part of why I've been rejecting you is to protect myself from you rejecting me. I don't feel like I can endure any more failure or rejection in my life.

I'm trying to reach out to you, or rather, to reach in. I can't make any promises except that I'll keep trying.

As I reflected, the abuse that I wanted to inflict on my younger self (but wasn't limited to my younger self) felt familiar. The feelings and actions echoed what I felt from my parents.

Once I realized that, I was indignant that this little girl was treated so unjustly. In an instant, I was her advocate instead of her abuser. Instead of working against myself, I became an ally.

Working with my inner child has been a key part of my healing. It's not enough to heal the damage of abuse; I also have to provide the nurturing care that I was denied. Reparenting myself does that.

I pay attention to the child within me. I listen to what is important to her and give her a voice. I address her fears by protecting her and comforting her. I provide the gentle treatment she never experienced.

I've reaped numerous benefits from connecting with my inner child:

- As I've taken better care of her, I've been able to take better care of my adult-self. Self-care has been one of the most challenging parts of my healing, but my success has been due to my relationship with my inner child.
- Reparenting myself has made me careful with my boundaries—especially with my parents. Even with my parents' continual abuse, my inner child still longed for a mommy and daddy. Her desperation to be nurtured and loved demolished her discernment. Providing her with the care that she needs has created less tension. She doesn't push me to restore the abusive relationship like she used to since her needs are met in me.
- Reparenting myself has protected my boundaries in another way. Even if I would subject myself to my parents' abuse, I'd never allow a child to have a

relationship with them. I can validate the feelings and desires of the child within me while protecting her. My adult self can withstand internal pressure that begs another chance out of my responsibility to the vulnerable part of me.

- Reparenting myself has restored a lot of my lost childhood. I give in to spontaneous urges to jump on the bed or spin across the room. By reuniting with my inner child, I'm free to be silly, to play and to explore. I can be the curious student rather than the wise teacher. The wonder of discovery has been restored—and with it, the wonder of life.
- I have a sense of being complete in myself that had been missing. I'm more in tune with myself; I'm in touch with my feelings and thoughts and I'm more accepting of all parts of me.

It's ironic that one of the major keys to feeling wholeness has been to think of my inner child as a separate person from me. But that's what I'd been doing all along. I separated from "her" to survive. Reuniting with this part of me is the foundation for the most important relationship of my life—my relationship with myself.

Over the years, I've continued to write as a way to reunite with my inner child. A key part is listening to her heart. One of the ways I listen is through writing letters to myself *from* my inner child. Experts suggest using the non-dominant hand for that, but I've found that typing works for me—perhaps because I'm using both hands.

> Dear Big Christina,
> I don't want to burden you but I don't know where I can go if you push me out. I'm so tired and afraid. I want to be held and loved. Mostly, I want to belong. Will you tell me that I belong with you?

Also, in response to the inner child exercise I did at the beginning of the chapter, I imagined myself as my inner child. I imagined what it felt like to be invited inside and cared for and finally having a home. The most impactful part of that for me was feeling seen. I felt recognized and known. After a lifetime of feeling invisible to my mother, that was powerfully healing.

Making a Home for Myself: Adopting My Inner Child

Suggested writing:

Write a letter from your inner child asking to come home.

The Rescued Soul

Write about your inner child knocking at your door. What do you feel? What do you do? What do you notice? Ask your inner child what he or she needs from you. What is your response?

Now write about you as your inner child showing up at your adult self's door. How do you feel?

Making a Home for Myself: Adopting My Inner Child

Write a letter to your inner child welcoming him or her home.

The Rescued Soul

6
Connecting With the Truth: Working Through a Memory

When I was a child, I was afraid of the dark. I was convinced that there were creatures lurking under my bed, in the closet, behind the chair. My parents appeased me by leaving the hall light on at night. In some ways that helped, but it illuminated my bedroom enough for me to see goblins in the shapes and shadows. I saw monsters peeking out from my not-quite-closed closet, waiting for me to fall asleep. I hid my head under the blankets, believing that the covers would be a monster shield.

I loved scary movies. I wasn't allowed to watch them since they were blamed for my fear, but my fear didn't come from something I saw; it came from my experience.

Though grown-ups didn't believe that monsters were real, I knew that they were. Horror films expressed what I couldn't—the reality of monsters. Through the movies, I could express the fear that never left me.

The part that frightened me the most was watching the girl curiously walk toward the strange noises. Her candle flickered, her companions disappeared, and still she crept forward. I always squirmed in my seat, yelling at the screen, willing her to turn around, "DON'T OPEN THAT DOOR!!!"

When it comes to facing my memories of my abuse, I'm the girl determined to seek out the unknown behind the door, but I'm also the audience member pleading with the girl to run in the opposite direction.

I recognize that the only way to stop being haunted from the ghosts of the past is to confront them. When something triggers me—a smell, a person, a situation, a touch, a place, a word—part of me is a Ghost-Buster, hunting down the things that threaten my peace. But when I walk down the dark corridor of a long-forgotten memory, another part of me wants to run away.

Before I'm even conscious of being triggered, the child within me fights as though it's a life and death struggle and screams, "You're going to die! Get away now!" To her, the trauma is ongoing and the threat is current. In that moment, it's not merely a memory, it's happening now.

In reality, it's not the yelling that hinders me, but something much quieter: The little girl in me defends herself in one of the only ways she ever could—

through dissociation, denial and repression. I crave food when I'm not hungry, I suddenly feel an overwhelming need for sleep, or I feel compelled to clean or to do some other kind of work—anything to escape.

From her perspective, everything is bigger and more powerful. Running away from perceived danger is her only option. She was never able to physically run away, but she escaped in her mind.

The trouble is, running away doesn't save me anymore; facing the memories so I can heal them is the only thing that can rescue me now.

My adult-self knows that if I'm triggered at all, I am ready to face those things. I may not feel ready, but just as my mind locked this away so long ago for my benefit, it's unlocking it at this time for my benefit.

The things I feel are what I would have felt during the abuse if I had been "present" enough to fully feel. It would have been too much for the child-me so I hid the feelings away for another time. And the time is now.

Even if I mentally will myself to pursue what dwells in the shadows of my mind, all my senses tell me it's too much for me. My child-self was all alone and never comforted during the original abuse and she (I) still needs nurturing support.

When I feel overwhelmed, I do things to comfort myself before I move forward:

- Deep breathing calms me. When I'm stressed I hold my breath, which creates more stress. Deep breathing gives me the nourishing oxygen my body needs and it helps me to focus on the here and now.
- Sometimes, I withdraw in solitude to feel safe and other times, I reach out to supportive friends. Alone or with someone else, I listen to myself with understanding and compassion and let myself be loved.
- I listen to my thoughts and feelings, whether they seem to make sense or not. Many times, I hear phrases that sound very juvenile. I recognize that they are feelings from the small child who never had a voice. Listening tells me that the things that happened to me really matter and that I matter.
- I write down what I remember. Many times, I don't feel any specific emotions until I write things out. There's something about seeing it on paper or on the screen that connects me to my feelings and I'm able to acknowledge them, express them and release them. Sometimes I can't cry, but it feels good to moan or to rock myself.

Once I comfort my inner child, I take her by the hand and we go through the door together. She shows me what happened there. I don't minimize or dismiss her experiences and fears like others have done to her and I used to do to her. I verify that they are every bit as awful as she believes them to be.

Connecting With the Truth: Working Through a Memory

My presence in her pain and fear allows her to join me in the present. My perspective shows her that the monsters are long gone and it's only the echoes from the past that we've been hearing. Behind the door, I don't find the death that I feared; I find my healing and my life.

Healing the Memories

Some people claim that digging up events that happened so long ago just keep us trapped there. On the contrary, looking at my past was the way to rescue myself from it. I was held captive by the beliefs and feelings of my abuse, but going back to examine them freed me.

Abuse is harmful in two ways: It damages us from the bad things that we weren't made to endure plus it denies us the vital things we needed to thrive. Healing deals with both of those things. It repairs the damage and provides the love and nurturing that were absent.

One of the key ways I was damaged from abuse was through the lies I came to believe about myself—mostly about my value. In every memory of my abuse, there are overt messages and covert messages. The *overt* messages come from things my abusers verbally communicated to me or about me. The *covert* messages come from what I deduced from the way I was being treated, rather than from actual words.

Sometimes, the memories seem to surface spontaneously. Other times, a current event in my life triggers a memory that still contains painful lies that I believe and live by. I've learned to pay attention to either feelings or behaviors that seem to be overreactions. Those are indicators of unresolved issues from the past. When I identify a possible trigger, I ask myself what that event reminded me of. When did I feel misunderstood like that? Or betrayed in a similar way? Or rejected? Immediately, the answer comes to mind.

Processing a Memory

This is a portion of one of my abuse memories and how I processed it:

When my dad was finished orally raping me, he threw my head off him in disgust. And then I was alone.

When I examine the original event, I ask myself some questions:

• What are the messages I believed about that?
• What does this tell me about myself? What does it say about my value?
• What did I learn about how I should expect to be treated?

The pain is coming from those lies that I believed.

Overt messages are things that the abuser verbalizes:

- Do you think you're the center of the universe?
- You'd make a good whore.
- Do you think you can do better than me?

Covert messages are communicated non-verbally:

- Nobody else will want you.
- Nobody cares about you.
- You're trash.
- You don't deserve to be loved.
- You don't deserve to be protected.
- You don't deserve to be comforted.

In that memory, I asked myself what I believed:

My dad's sudden thrust of my head seemed to demand, "How could you???" as though he were the victim of the rape. My dad couldn't wait to get away from me. That told me I was shameful. I was to blame for what happened to me. The only touch I was worthy to receive is sexual touch and I'm even too dirty for that. I deserve to be alone. No one should have to contaminate himself with my presence.

Every trauma experience communicates some specific lie that we believe and live by until we confront it with the truth. In this case, these are truths that I used to debunk the lies:

I was just a little girl. I couldn't be to blame for something that my dad did TO me. Something bad was done to me; I'm not bad. My dad's urgency to flee from me was because of HIS shame. It was HIS action, not mine. I don't deserve to be abandoned.

I walk through the memory as though I'm reliving it. The more difficult it is to face, the greater the impact it has in my life. Some of the more painful memories require me to take a break before I process all of it, but knowing that facing it will greatly improve my life, I'm motivated to press on when I'm ready.

Sometimes, the abuse itself doesn't bring up much emotion, but feelings emerge when I consider the messages behind the actions. I sit with my emotions and express them in whatever way I need to. I cry, write, call a friend, or cuddle up in a blanket. I acknowledge that my feelings are valid and important.

Connecting With the Truth: Working Through a Memory

I also grieve the loss. The lies caused me to behave in ways that stole the life I could have lived. I missed opportunities, I sabotaged myself, I stayed in abusive relationships, I didn't raise my children the way I wish I had. I express the anger and sadness over the ways I adapted to the abuse. Grief opens the door to new possibilities.

My memory brings up these losses:

> *I adapted to feeling filthy in so many ways. I couldn't stand to be touched. I was afraid of contaminating people and of being contaminated even more. I'm a germaphobe. For a long time, I couldn't even feel the pleasure of touch that wasn't sexual. When my kids were little, I resisted cuddling with them because I hated touch and because I believed the only touch was sexual touch.*

As I'm doing memory work, I stay conscious of what I'm feeling. Having the urge to jump up and do something else, or to escape in some other way, is an indication that I need to slow down and comfort myself. Staying present and allowing the pain to surface is one of the most compassionate things I can do for myself. It's a message to myself that I'm worthy of love and that I don't deserve to be abandoned.

As I relive a memory:

- I pay attention to the overt and covert messages.
- I confront the lies with the truth.
- I express my emotions about the event, about the lies and about the ways the lies have influenced my life.
- I grieve the losses that I see in my life that came from the ways I adapted to the abuse.
- I give myself the comfort and understanding that I didn't receive after the trauma.

Suggested writing:

What are some ways you can comfort yourself as you're doing memory work?

41

What is a memory you have from your childhood that still causes you pain? If you don't know where to start, start with when you were youngest. Write out what happened.

What are the overt messages you received? Did your abuser say anything to you?

Connecting With the Truth: Working Through a Memory

What are the covert messages you received? What did the way you were treated communicate to you?

What do you feel about how you were treated and what you thought or think about yourself?

The Rescued Soul

How did those lies influence your life? How do you feel about that?

7
Connecting to Myself by Writing My Story

Before I started healing, I was living out of my parents' version of my story. According to their version, I was spoiled and strong-willed and would lie and do whatever I needed just to get attention. I came from a very good family who loved me and did everything they could for me, yet somehow, I turned out bad.

That's the story that I believed about myself until my healing process prompted me to question the "reality" that I "knew". Telling my own story was a powerful way to take back my life.

Before I compiled my story, I felt disjointed as a person. My past was in little scraps, disconnected and without context. Telling my story was the beginning of understanding myself. The fragments of my past fit together, which helped me feel more "put together" than I ever had. I went from feeling dismembered to remembered. Instead of being stuck in my abuse, clearly seeing my past helped me to finally begin to move away from it.

I assembled my history by writing my story from beginning to end (as far as I knew it). This is what I wrote:

> I don't remember thinking about sexual abuse until I was about fourteen or fifteen. I was dating a boy and told him I had been raped. It seemed strange to me since I didn't have any memory of being raped and hadn't planned to say that. It came out of my mouth before I really thought about it. When I heard myself say that, I realized I had the feeling for a long time that something awful had happened to me and that I felt dirty.
>
> When I was in my early twenties, I drove past a preschool in a neighborhood close to where I lived as a young child. Suddenly, I knew I'd been sexually abused. I didn't remember a specific instance, but I knew it was a fact, not just a feeling.
>
> For years, I couldn't remember anything specific. I knew that it was my dad who had abused me. I don't know how I knew, but I knew. But also thought I might have been abused by others. I had the feeling of being passed around.
>
> Although I didn't have any specific memories, I could identify some of the effects of the abuse. I had difficulty setting boundaries, I had problems saying no to men, I acted in a very seductive way, and I was full of shame.

45

Years passed and my twenty-one year marriage to a man who was verbally and financially abusive ended.

Five years later, I was happily and safely remarried and then everything changed. My twenty-four year old daughter, Bethany, called me one night to tell me she wanted to report her father, my ex-husband, for sexually abusing her. I started having graphic flashbacks and dreams about my own abuse. I started seeing my childhood memories in a different light. All along, I thought I had no memories of my abuse, but it slowly occurred to me that what I thought of as normal father and daughter activities were in reality acts of sexual abuse.

I had minimized one of them by just calling it "strange" and "hurtful":

When I was about eight or nine years old, I was playing dress up with my mom's things as my parents were entertaining guests. I put on my mom's black half slip and wore it as a dress. I accessorized it with her shoes and pearls. I felt pretty and wanted to show everyone. I was too afraid of rejection to go into the family room, where all the adults were so I passed by them on the way to the front patio. As I was going outside, my dad said to the guests that I would make a good call girl. Everyone laughed. I felt a strange mixture of pride and shame. Somehow, I knew that my dad approved of me "making a good call girl," but I also knew there was badness attached to it.

The flashbacks, nightmares and other memories revealed that my father not only abused me himself, but also traded me to other men. He took me to sex parties where young children were exchanged. My dad sent me to the neighbor's house, where the neighbor raped me with a pool cue in his basement. I walked home alone, hoping nobody would see what a bad girl I was.

The things I wrote were the things that seemed important to me at the time. I started with the first time I suspected that I had been sexually abused and most of my story is the chronology of my discoveries. I wasn't conscious of it at the time, but the thing that was most important to me then wasn't the abuse itself, but how I remembered it. I was still struggling to believe that it could be real. Assembling my history helped me to confirm what I already knew, but still needed to accept. It helped me to believe myself.

My story and the way I see it continues to grow and change as I do. My story doesn't end with the abuse. Today, my story is not complete without including my healing.

My revised story:

I was afraid every day of my childhood. I don't remember a time when it wasn't a struggle. I struggled to fit in. I struggled to be good enough. I struggled to figure how to make people like me. Life was hard.

Connecting to Myself by Writing My Story

I came from a family of four. My mom stayed home with my brother and me until we were older. My dad had lots of different jobs: golf pro, business owner, office manager, bartender, truck driver, handyman and others. We seemed like a normal family. We took vacations together, we celebrated holidays together and we ate dinner together. All the time we lived together, we were emotionally distant from each other. Virtual strangers.

I don't remember how young I was when my dad first sexually abused me. Most of the sexual abuse that I remember comes from the time I was eight or nine, though I know he abused me before and after those years.

I didn't always remember my abuse—at least not consciously. I repressed most of it until I was an adult. It came back over a period of years. When the memories returned, they didn't seem real. They felt a lot like dreams or like those things happened to someone else. The only things that seemed real about them were the intense fear that came with them and how they all tied together. There was something very familiar about them. They fit.

Even though I forgot most of my abuse, there were a few things that I never forgot. I didn't define them as sexually abusive until I learned the true definition of sexual abuse.

I had minimized them by just calling those things, "strange" and "hurtful":

When I was about eight or nine years old, I was playing dress up with my mom's things as my parents were entertaining guests. I put on my mom's black half slip and wore it as a dress. I accessorized it with her shoes and pearls. I felt pretty and wanted to show everyone. I was too afraid of rejection to present myself to the adults so I passed by them on the way to the front patio, hoping they would see me. As I was going outside, my dad joked to the guests that I would make a good call girl. Everyone laughed. I felt a strange mixture of pride and shame. Somehow, I knew that my dad approved of me "making a good call girl" but I also knew there was badness attached to it.

Another part of my sexual abuse that I always remembered but tried not to think about was that my dad liked to watch me masturbate. He'd get a glazed look in his eyes, like he was sexually aroused. I remember feeling uncomfortable about it, but my dad really liked it and he gave me his approval.

The way I seemed able to earn my dad's approval and "love" was through sexual acts. It seemed impossible to earn approval or love from my mother so my dad was my only hope not to be abandoned.

Even though I didn't remember most of my abuse or define the things that I did remember as abuse, I still suffered the effects of it. Among the effects that I was most conscious of, I felt shameful and dirty. I grew up feeling different from everyone else, as though I didn't deserve to belong. I was terribly alone, no matter how many people were in my life.

47

When I was married to my first husband, he told me that he'd been sexually abused by his parents. I was devastated, as though it had happened to me. Soon after that, I began to remember that I had been sexually abused. It was more than just a suspicion; I knew.

Many years passed. I divorced my husband and discovered that he had molested our daughter almost all of her childhood. Sexual abuse was again in the forefront of my mind. I started having graphic flashbacks and dreams.

The flashbacks, nightmares and other memories revealed that my father not only abused me himself, but also traded me to other men. He took me to sex parties where young children were exchanged. My dad sent me to the neighbor's house, where the neighbor raped me with a pool cue in his basement.

It was hard to accept those things as real, but they kept coming up. All of them seemed to have a common theme of betrayal and violation. As hard as it was to accept, it was hard to deny that they fit all that I'd felt my whole life and the ways I behaved.

It's taken me about six years to get to where I am now. By addressing the worst part of my life, I made it possible to live the best part of my life. Even though those things happened to me, they don't define me. My life is far more than the abuse. I've faced the fear, the pain and the anger from the ways I was treated and those old memories don't haunt me anymore. The effects of the abuse—the ways I coped—are fading. I'm delighted with the person I am. I'm surrounded by people who value me the way I value myself. I'm thrilled with the life I have!

Suggested writing:

Has someone else written a story about your life? It's your life and it's your story. You're the only one who can tell the truth about you. Are you ready to write your own story? There is no right or wrong way to do this, but here are some ideas for getting started:

- What was the context of your abuse? What was going on in your life at the time? What was it like to be you at the age(s) when the abuse occurred?
- What was your family of origin like? What was you relationship with your family members?
- Do you remember life before you were abused?
- Who abused you? What was your relationship to the abuser?
- What did the abuser do to you?
- How did the abuse change you?

Connecting to Myself by Writing My Story

Write as much as you remember and include the details that are significant to you. Take as much time as you need. You might need time to think about what you want to say. You aren't bound to what you write, either. You can create a new version as you create a new life for yourself.

The Rescued Soul

Connecting to Myself by Writing My Story

The Rescued Soul

When you're finished writing your story, read it to yourself.

- Does anything about it stand out to you? Are you surprised by anything?

- How do you feel?

- How do you feel about the child that those things were perpetrated on?

- How would you feel if those things happened to another child? What if they happened to your child?

If writing a story is too difficult right now, try to make a list of the things you remember.

8
Connecting to Myself by Writing a Fictional Story

The sun was falling behind the trees, the wind was gusting. The child desperately sought refuge, though not from the elements. The man was getting closer, the same man who had hurt her before in ways she couldn't understand.

The girl spotted movement in one of the houses. A woman was inside, cheerful watering the dozen or so plants that hung at her window.

The small fists banged on the door, "Let me in…Help me, PLEEEE-ASE!" Getting no reply, the child ran to the window, frantically motioning for the woman's attention. Seemingly oblivious to the sobbing child's face pressed outside the glass, the woman continued humming to herself.

With nowhere else to go, the little girl tried to hide, willing herself to be invisible, hoping the danger would pass if she stayed quiet and still. As she crouched in her makeshift refuge, the man was beside her, hovering, reaching down…

Every time I write a fictional story about a child being abused, I understand more of my own story. Writing fiction draws details about my abuse I didn't realize that I knew about my experience, beliefs and feelings.

The story above was an expression of my desperation for my mother to see me. At the time I wrote that, the child within me still cried out to be seen and heard. Writing is one of the ways I provide her with the validation and understanding that she needs.

The first time I wrote about a little girl abused by her father—actually a short screenplay (included at the end of this chapter), I didn't intend for it to be autobiographical. I was merely "writing what I know". I came to a scene where the child was lying in bed, listening for her tormentor's footsteps. I was flooded with an overwhelming sense of isolation. When nobody else was around, *he* could get me. I wasn't only physically alone—unprotected—I was completely without an ally. There was nowhere to run, nobody to hear my cries for help, nobody to believe me or comfort me. In the whole wide world of people, I was deserted.

The Rescued Soul

Though painful, that was a breakthrough for me. I needed to really feel my aloneness and grieve it. I couldn't stop *being* alone until I acknowledged how alone I really had been.

Fictional writing is an effective way to access the unconscious mind. That's why I was unaware that I was actually writing about myself, yet I still communicated a profound truth.

The last piece of fiction I wrote, a fairy tale, was one I resisted working on. After some time, I realized that my reluctance came from feeling the vulnerability of a child again. I felt silly and childish to use my imagination that way. Writing in a fantasy genre threatened my need to feel strong and in control.

Once I understood my fear, I validated it and reassured myself that I was safe. Seeing how much I fought it, I concluded that there was something important to face. Having finished my story, I'm not sure which part was a more valuable piece of the assignment: the insight I faced in starting it or in finishing it.

Writing fiction draws details about my abuse I didn't even realize that I knew. Stories are powerful because they reveal truth.

MONSTERS AREN'T REAL

FADE IN

INT. MASTER BEDROOM - NIGHT

Soft light filters in the window from a street light, illuminating two figures on the bed. ABBY, thirty-three, and JAKE, thirty-six, sleep peacefully with long, slow breathing.

From another room, a CHILD'S MUFFLED SCREAM breaks the quiet.

Abby starts awake and jumps to her feet in a quick, urgent motion. Jake grunts slightly and rolls over, barely conscious of anything around him. His eyes close again.

Abby runs from the room.

INT. CAITLIN'S ROOM - CONTINUOUS ACTION

Abby rushes through the door. Ranks of stuffed animals stare down from their perches on a dresser and shelves above a small desk. The furniture rests against yellow polka dotted wallpaper and pink ruffled curtains.

Abby flicks frantically at the light switch as she passes on her way to the bed.

                    ABBY
          Caitlin?

The light pops on and the screaming, emanating from a mound of covers on the small bed, stops instantly, as though the switch is attached to it.

Abby sits on the side of the bed and pulls the covers back.

The frightened face of eight-year-old CAITLIN stares out from beneath the tangle of blankets and sheets. Trembling arms pull the blankets close under her chin. Her eyes blink at the sudden influx of light.

> ABBY
> Caitlin, Sweetie, it's
> just a dream.

Caitlin pulls the blankets closer, disbelieving. Beads of sweat speckle her forehead.

Abby brushes her hand over Caitlin's forehead.

> ABBY
> Caitlin, you're soaked.

She pulls at the blankets to loosen them from Caitlin's grip. They slide away, revealing a heavy coat zipped up to Caitlin's neck.

> ABBY
> What are you wearing?

Caitlin stares, wide eyes, no answer.

Abby pulls Caitlin toward her and hugs her.

> ABBY
> Why are you wearing your
> coat?

> CAITLIN
> So they won't get me.

Abby leans back and looks into Caitlin's face, brushing sweat-matted hair back from her little forehead.

Connecting to Myself by Writing a Fictional Story

> ABBY
> Sweetie, there's nothing
> to be afraid of. Monsters
> aren't real.

INT. MASTER BEDROOM - NIGHT

Abby slides back into bed next to Jake. He grunts
again in response to the bed shaking and rolls over
to look at her.

> JAKE
> She okay?

Abby nods.

> JAKE
> Maybe I'll take her to
> the Pier tomorrow. She's
> been asking to go.

> ABBY
> She'll love that.

She rolls over, facing away from him.

He reaches his hand to her shoulder and rubs it re-
assuringly.

> JAKE
> You okay?

She pauses, as though unsure how to answer.

> ABBY
> I don't know if I'll be
> able to go back to sleep.

He reaches around her and pulls her closer.

The Rescued Soul

JAKE
Let me help you relax.

INT. KITCHEN - NIGHT

Abby moves dishes around the counter, stacking them
in preparation for putting them away.

The door flies open with a bang as Caitlin bursts
through, carrying a twisted balloon. Jake stumbles
in behind her.

CAITLIN
Mommy, we're home.

Abby turns toward her and kneels to Caitlin's eye
level.

ABBY
Did you have fun?

CAITLIN
We went on the Ferris
wheel, and the swing-
ing dragon thing. Daddy,
what's that called?

Jake shrugs his shoulders.

JAKE
It's a -- a swinging
dragon thing.

CAITLIN
Oh, yeah. And I got sick
cause I ate a hot dog
right before I rode the
dragon. But I didn't
throw up, though. I just
had to sit down a little

while. But that's okay,
cause then there was a
bubble machine, and I ran
through the bubbles and
popped them, and I got em
in my hair, and I got one
in my mouth, and it was
yucky.

                ABBY
        Sounds like you had a
        good time. But it's way
        past your bedtime. Give
        me a hug, and off you go.

Caitlin holds up the balloon, twisted into the shape
of a dog.

                CAITLIN
        But I didn't show you my
        puppy. The monster gave
        it to me.

Abby's glance darts at Jake, a thinly veiled glare.

                ABBY
        Jake?

                CAITLIN
        It's okay, Mommy. He
        wasn't a scary monster.
        He had a long nose and
        his eyes popped out. He
        was a funny monster.

Abby sighs and struggles to regain a pleasant expression.

                    ABBY
          That's nice. You can tell
          me the rest when I tuck
          you in. Now give your
          daddy a kiss and brush
          your teeth.

Caitlin backs away slightly, her expression changing
suddenly from excited to solemn.

                    CAITLIN
          I'm not tired.

Abby gives Caitlin a stern expression.

                    ABBY
          Caitlin Jane!

Caitlin pops over to kiss her dad and mopes off.

                    JAKE
          I love you, Beautiful.

INT. CAITLIN'S ROOM - NIGHT

Caitlin lies in bed, covers up to her eyes.

Abby walks in and stops. She sees a line of colored
glitter on the floor, snaking around the bed like a
rough boundary marker.

                    ABBY
          Caitlin, what is this?

                    CAITLIN
          It's magic dust.

Abby furrows her brow, attempting to look serious.

                    CAITLIN
          To keep the monsters out.

                    ABBY
          Sweetie, monsters aren't
          real.

Caitlin stares back, clearly sceptical.

                    ABBY
          Mommy and Daddy are right
          down the hall. Nothing's
          gonna hurt you.

                    CAITLIN
          Would you check?

Abby sighs and stands, reluctantly walking through
the motions of a familiar ritual. She opens the
closet door, makes a pretense of looking inside,
then turns back toward Caitlin.

                    ABBY
          No monsters.

She kneels next to Caitlin and pulls up the bed
skirt, peering briefly underneath.

                    ABBY
          Nope, nothing here.

She stands and faces Caitlin again. Caitlin points
to the window.

Abby walks slowly to the pink ruffled curtains and
pulls them back, one at a time.

                    ABBY
          All clear.

She crosses her arms and faces the bed, eyebrows
raised, waiting. Caitlin stares for a moment.

> CAITLIN
> Turn them away.

She looks at the rows of stuffed animals on the dresser and the shelves. Abby moves to the shelf and turns all the animals toward the wall, one by one, working her way from left to right.

> ABBY
> Now are you happy?

Caitlin looks around the room, inspecting the preparations.

> CAITLIN
> Can I sleep with you?

Abby sits on the bed again.

> ABBY
> No, Sweetie, you're a big
> girl now -- and monsters
> aren't real.

Abby kisses Caitlin on the forehead, stands, and turns a night light on.

> ABBY
> Sweet dreams.

She flicks the light off and ducks out of the room.

INT. MASTER BEDROOM - NIGHT

Abby lies in her bed, eyes closed, deep regular breathing. The bed next to her is empty.

Connecting to Myself by Writing a Fictional Story

INT. CAITLIN'S ROOM - NIGHT

Caitlin stirs from her sleep at the low sound of a
CREAK from the floor. She looks up as Jake walks qui-
etly into the room and closes the door behind him.

Caitlin's eyes close again as she pulls the covers
up to her face. She hears the sound of CRUNCHING as
a footstep crushes the line of magic powder. Caitlin's breathing almost stops.

> CAITLIN
> Monsters aren't real.
> Monsters aren't real.
> Monsters aren't real.

A shadow crosses her face.

FADE OUT.

Suggested writing:

Are you willing to write a fictional story based on your abuse? There is no right or wrong way to do this, but here are some ideas for getting started:

- What is the setting? Where does it take place? When does it take place? Is it a realistic world or a fantasy world?

- Who are the main characters? Are they people, animals, plants or some other type of creatures? What are their names? Who is the main character? Who is the villain?

- What happens to harm the main character? How does that affect the character? What does he/she do?

- How does the main character overcome the harm?

No matter where you are in your healing journey, finish your story with a happy ending. It's important to imagine a positive outcome for your life. You never had a choice of how your life started, but you have a choice in how it ends.

Connecting to Myself by Writing a Fictional Story

The Rescued Soul

The Rescued Soul

When you're finished writing your fictional story, read it to yourself.

- Does anything about it stand out to you? Are you surprised by anything?

- Is there some part of the story that seems to be more important for you to communicate?

- How do you feel?

9
Connecting With Others by Sharing My Story

I'd repressed most of my childhood memories when suddenly, in my early twenties, I knew I'd been sexually abused. The knowledge came in a flash. Before that, all I'd had were suspicions and vague feelings but in that moment, the fog lifted. I didn't have any specific recall, or know who my abuser was, but I was *sure* I'd been abused.

Naively, I turned to my parents. I thought they could help me fill in the blanks. When I walked in their house, my mom stood in the kitchen. We made small talk for a few minutes and then I calmly stated, "I was sexually abused." I heard a booming voice from the next room, where my dad was watching television, "NO, YOU WEREN'T!!!" My mother didn't respond at all. It was as though I'd never said a word.

At that time, I was still very disconnected from my pain. I wasn't looking for support; I was only looking for answers. I wanted to know what happened to me. My parent's reaction told me I wouldn't get any help from them.

In the years that followed, I remembered more. It was my dad who sexually abused me while my mom looked the other way. In that light, their responses to my disclosure made so much sense. I didn't know it then, but now I know that telling my parents wasn't the best place to begin talking about my abuse.

To cope with the abuse, I'd made up an idealized image of my family. To minimize my sense of abandonment and betrayal, I'd imagined that they were loving and supportive. That fantasy blinded me to the truth until I was ready to face it.

As the truth started to return, so did the pain. I began to connect the incest with some of my behaviors. I needed more than answers to my past; I needed healing from it.

A few years after telling my parents, I was validated by a group of women who openly discussed their own abuse. They believed me and supported me. Through their example and encouragement, I started to see that healing was possible.

Taking the First Steps in Telling

What I didn't know when I disclosed my abuse is that it's very common for families to reject rather than support the survivor. That's especially true with incest survivors. In incest families, the family system is a culture that protects itself by keeping the secret. That system's survival depends on the secret, so they often sacrifice one member for the sake of the family.

In most cases, the survivor who is willing to talk about the abuse is the healthiest person in the family. The survivor is the one who recognizes the truth and is most motivated to address dysfunctional patterns. That is a threat to the family unit. The person who wants change is often viewed and treated as the enemy.

With incest, family members face divided loyalties. In dysfunctional families, it's more common to side with the perpetrator than with the victim. That may be due to their own victimization from the perpetrator or unmet needs from the perpetrator. Whatever the cause, survivors of incest are often rejected by their own family members, even if there is no doubt the abuse occurred.

Sometimes parents reject the possibility that their child was abused because to accept the truth is too painful. Sometimes the disclosure brings up pain from their own abuse. They also may view it as an accusation that they aren't good parents for failing to protect their child.

Whatever the personal defenses, your family isn't likely to be the best source of support and understanding. Telling a safe person who validates you makes it easier to go on to the next part of your healing. When you disclose your abuse to someone who is compassionate, understanding, and accepting, it's a relief to know you're no longer alone. However, sharing emotionally vulnerable moments with someone who is unsupportive may cause you to feel even more isolated.

When choosing a person to tell, consider:

- Someone who is comfortable with discussing emotional issues and who doesn't try to control your emotions
- Someone who isn't opinionated or judgmental
- Someone you already feel safe with—someone you've shared other private information with and has earned your trust
- Someone who doesn't know your abuser or who isn't emotionally (or otherwise) invested in a relationship with your abuser

These are some things to remember to increase the chances that your disclosure will be well-received:

Connecting With Others by Sharing My Story

- Prepare the person by telling them you have something important to talk about and schedule a time that will allow both of you time to deal with your emotions.
- Start small and privately.
- Evaluate your emotions and practice self-care after each new step in disclosure.
- Take time to validate yourself after you disclose.
- If you want to make your abuse experience known to more people or disclose to your family, establish a base of support with trusted others first.

No matter how anyone responds, what happened to you was serious and you deserve to be treated well. Don't allow anyone to keep you from doing what's best for you. You may not get the validation you need from everyone, but you can validate yourself.

The Benefits of Sharing
Despite the risks, talking about your abuse also has its rewards:

- My experience was denied by others and by me, but telling my story acknowledged the truth. It was difficult to deny my abuse once I revealed the secret.
- As I talked about my past, I came to accept that it really happened—and it didn't just happen, it happened to *me*. I went over it again and again—in my mind and with others. This wasn't a television show or news story—this was *my* story.
- Abuse is devaluing. Talking about it is a declaration to myself that I'm important and what happened to me really matters.
- Talking about my abuse allows me to hear myself. As I listen, I hear myself emphasize details that I'd thought were insignificant. It's given me greater understanding of my feelings and behaviors today. I've make connections between past events and current feelings and behaviors. I've solved today's problems by looking back at how I got here.
- Talking to understanding and compassionate people was the gateway to feeling compassion for myself and acknowledging the depth of my loss. When I finally sat still with my experience and listened to my heart, I finally *felt* heard. The horror and tears on a friend's face told me that what happened to me really was bad and that I wasn't making a big deal out of nothing.
- Every time I talked about my abuse, I freed myself of more of the fear of breaking the secret.

- Telling was a way to break free from the bond the secret created between me and my abusers. I felt less captive to my abusers' power.
- Shame thrives in secrecy. Talking about my abuse helped to cast off the shame.
- Releasing the secret in this area helped me live more freely in other areas. I didn't have to guard every word as though I'd accidentally say something about the abuse.
- As long as I held onto the secret, I also held onto the pain. Sharing helped me access the feelings so I could release the pain in the comforting company of a witness.
- Abuse is isolating. Sharing the truth about my past has been a way to connect with others. Having feedback from others heals the pain of isolation and makes support possible.
- Telling the truth often leads to more truth. Telling helped me recover new memories and helped me make connections with other memories.
- Keeping the secret protects the abusers. By sharing my story, I moved from the lifestyle of protecting my abusers to protecting myself.

Talking about my abuse was an important part of reclaiming myself so I could move forward. Talking about my past didn't keep me there; it allowed me to move out of it.

Even after I'd been talking about my abuse for years, taking new steps opened new depths of feelings. One of my last steps was a radio interview. It felt natural and comfortable to speak openly but the next day, I felt exhausted and defeated. As I heard myself talk about my abuse, I accepted and understood it at a deeper level. I accessed new layers of grief I hadn't touched before. It was painful, but I was glad to be taking another step in my healing.

Take time to evaluate how you feel after each new disclosure step. Those feelings need to be validated and expressed. Emotions are good, even if they're painful. Just as in all parts of the healing process, it's important to take small steps and proceed at your own rate.

Connecting With Others by Sharing My Story

Suggested writing:

How do you feel about disclosing your abuse? Have you talked about it yet? Who have you shared it with? If you shared it, how did the other person respond?

If you haven't told anyone about your abuse, who do you know who would be likely to receive it well? Make a list based on the list above and evaluate it from you head and heart.

The Rescued Soul

10
Connecting With Others: Overcoming the Fear of Telling

For a long time after I started talking about my abuse, I felt guilty for not speaking up sooner. I didn't believe I really had a right to complain about my abuse since I hadn't complained about it while it was going on. If I hated it so much, why didn't I say something then? I felt like I was changing the rules in the middle of the game. I'd played by them all my life so it seemed unfair to stop after so long.

It didn't seem as though it could have been so hard to tell someone that my dad was hurting me. I thought I must have either been a very stupid or weak child or that I must not have wanted the abuse to stop.

As an adult, I wanted to scream at my child-self, "JUST TELL!!!" I was blaming the little girl I had been for all my pain. I thought if she would have just pushed a little harder, she could have saved me.

There was one time I specifically remember that I had a chance to disclose my abuse. I was ten years old and a psychologist from the school district pulled me out of class after observing students for a few days. I knew she had singled me out because there was something wrong with me. I already felt like I had some kind of sign on me that told everyone that I was bad and disgusting. On one hand, I was screaming inside, "DON'T LOOK AT ME!!!" On the other hand, I was pleading, "Notice me!"

The psychologist asked me why I seemed sad and I struggled for an answer. I didn't relate my sadness to what my dad was doing to me. I didn't even consider that those things weren't normal. I tried to come up with the "right" answer, so I told her I didn't have any friends. That wasn't really true. I had playmates, but I felt all alone.

The woman seemed disappointed and annoyed with me. I didn't know what she wanted or expected, but I wasn't doing something right. She worked with me and taught me social skills for a few months and then I was on my own again.

I felt like the whole world was against me so reaching out for help didn't seem like a possibility. I thought I deserved bad things. I didn't have hope for my life being any *less* painful so I focused on not making it any *more* painful.

Even though I judged myself for not figuring out how I could be saved, I can see now that I was very smart in some ways. During those years of incest and other abuses, I learned to read people very well so I could prepare myself for what was coming. Without knowing how I knew, I knew certain people weren't safe.

Looking back, nothing about that psychologist told me that I could trust her. She seemed to view me as a project rather than a person. I had the feeling she was more interested in her own success than in truly helping me. I couldn't trust this stranger, but why couldn't I trust my mom? Why didn't I tell her?

Even after everything my mother had done to me as an adult, a part of me still believed in the fairy tale image I'd carried of her in childhood. I believed that something had made her change from the loving mother grew up with into a distant, verbally violent accuser.

In a threatening letter she sent to me after I publically disclosed my abuse, I realized that I didn't have a mother—not just now that I'd told my secret, but that I'd never had a mom who loved and supported me. She hadn't recently turned her back on me. She was treating me the way she always had.

That showed me another perspective. The closest thing to love I had as a little girl was from my dad. Even if I had to trade my body for a little attention and affection, my dad was the only source of anything that resembled love. Even though I didn't like what he was doing to me, I felt more security from him than I did from my mom. Telling wasn't an option when I was being abused since the punishment for breaking my silence was that I would be completely abandoned by both of my parents.

Examining the past has shown me the truth about myself and about my abuse. I wasn't to blame for not telling someone about my abuse when I was a child. I was doing my job, which was to survive. I listened to my intuition and protected myself from more pain.

I wasn't being unfair to break the "no telling" rule. Keeping the secret so I could survive wasn't the same as agreeing to the rules. Compliance isn't agreement. It *was* unfair to be abused and neglected in my own home and then to be expected to cover it up. I had every right to start playing by my own rules—rules that are based on equality, not on my abusers being the only ones who could ever win.

Internal and External Warnings

The first time I spoke about my sexual abuse publicly, it was to a group of about forty people. Most of the people in the group knew my father so I was nervous about their response. Despite the possible negative reactions, I felt ready to share it. I had enough of a support system, within myself and with others, so I was secure with the truth.

Connecting With Others: Overcoming the Fear of Telling

Surprisingly, my disclosure was very well received. Several people approached me afterward to tell me about their own abuse. They appreciated my vulnerability and courage. It inspired them to begin healing.

I was validated by the group but when I went home that night I heard a little girl's voice in my head saying, "You told!," in an accusing tone. I recognized that the voice belonged to the little girl inside of me. She was the one whose world would have been upended by exposing the secret. She was the one who was warned not to tell.

Fear gripped me and I was a child again, at the mercy of my parents along with their judgment and the abandonment that went with it. As my adult self, I comforted my inner child with a reminder that I wasn't under my parents' power anymore.

I continued to talk openly about the things my dad did to me and the things he let other men do to me. After a couple of years of sharing my story publicly, I didn't have much internal backlash. However, I didn't know how much that old fear of getting in trouble still haunted me. I hadn't had contact with my parents during that time, though I'd heard from a few people that they didn't like what I was saying. Then I got a certified letter from my mother:

Jan. 31, 2011
Christina-

I am writing to inform you that your malicious slander of your father has not gone unnoticed. You have built an entire world out of your fantasy. In dreaming up your sexual abuse you have maligned your father's character and deeply hurt his heart and mine. Your lies shall surely catch up with you.

I want you to know that if you have any plans of writing a book, we will sue you and anyone who has anything to do with it. Your defamation of your father's character will stop. You will not enjoy one penny from any book published about this gross lie.

And I should let you know that we filed some of your inflammatory statements about your father and me, along with your threat against me, with the Mesa Police Dept.

And I will always be your mother whether you recognize me or not as such.
Your mother-
[name withheld]

When I got this, there were two voices in my head. I heard my adult voice, who had healed enough to see the truth behind the threats. I also heard the voice of the little girl inside of me who was still vulnerable to abuse and rejection. I had to dissect this letter to face my fears and to recognize the lies behind them.

77

The Rescued Soul

"I'm writing to inform you…"

The way my mom phrased that statement was so impersonal, as if to emphasize her distance from me. My mom distanced herself from me all my life and this was a painful reminder of that. Though this line didn't appear to be a threat, it served as a threat to my child-self. Even though they'd already walked away from me a few years before, it was a reminder of the original abandonment of childhood that said, "You're not good enough to be around us, so get in line or we won't love you anymore. You'll be all alone in the world and nobody will ever love you."

The fear of abandonment forced me to comply as a child, but I'm not forced to comply anymore. The key people in my life did reject me for telling the truth, but I'm not alone. Even if the consequence for telling the truth is rejection from everyone I know, that's not the same death threat that it was when I was a child. I'm a self-sufficient adult and abandonment no longer means the end of my life.

Actually, separation from my abusers brought me a much more affirming life. Being away from my parents for a few years showed me I could live very easily and happily without them. I just needed to reassure my child-self of that.

"I'm writing to inform you that your malicious slander of your father has not gone unnoticed."

The little girl inside of me panicked. "Oh no! They don't like what I'm doing and they caught me telling." I'd learned from my family that it was acceptable for them to violate my innocence, but it was unforgivable for me to talk about the violation. But I don't live by those incest family values anymore. I didn't do anything wrong by talking about the things my dad did to me.

"Malicious slander" sounded so evil. It was that same fear of being labeled "bad". That's a huge part of my need to follow the rules. Being treated like trash gave me the message I was trash so I tried to be perfect as a way out of the shame. Even though I'd dealt with the majority of that, I still needed to assure myself that I'm not the bad one here. I carried my dad's shame for what he did to me long enough. I wasn't the one who had done anything wrong—he was.

"You have built an entire world out of your fantasy."

When I first started talking about my abuse, it felt like I was lying. I didn't feel connected to what I knew. It all felt distant and surreal, like a dream. Added to that, I didn't have any emotions about it for a long time. It was as though it happened to someone else. It didn't seem possible to experience such horrible things and not feel anything about it, so on some level, it felt like I was making it up. Eventually, the emotions came and I knew those things happened to me.

Connecting With Others: Overcoming the Fear of Telling

Even though I couldn't be shaken from the truth anymore, my mother's claim that I was making this up was crushing. I'd felt invisible to my mother my whole life and now she was tossing me aside with the same dismissive attitude. "Your abuse didn't exist and neither do you."

In my mind, I was a small child standing before my mother, pleading for her protection and comfort. Not being believed or acknowledged was life threatening then, but I acknowledge my own life through my healing and I don't need her to believe me now. Coming face to face with this pain showed me what validation I needed to give to myself.

"In dreaming up your sexual abuse you have maligned your father's character and deeply hurt his heart and mine."

In their twisted world, they are the victims and I am their abuser. This kind of manipulative guilt trip used to work on me. I was trained to take care of their feelings in the hope that if they were fulfilled, they'd finally take care of me. I waited for the validation for most of my life that my needs were important too, but it never came from them. Their manipulations stopped working when I realized my value and stopped needing their permission to put myself first.

"Your lies shall surely catch up with you."

I heard this as, "It's not only your dad and me who will act in opposition to you, but powers bigger than us will overpower you and you'll be sorry you ever crossed us." That struck such a nerve and I realized that I'd always been afraid of that. I had an unconscious fear that God or some other force would punish me for talking about my abuse. Sometimes while I was driving, I was sure another driver would be an instrument in the universe's hand to pronounce judgment on me. I was afraid I'd discover some gruesome disease overtaking my body. I was always on guard, never knowing which direction retribution would come from.

I'd pushed that fear aside and dismissed it as silly, but reading my mother's words showed me just how much power that lie still had over me. As a child, my parents were gods to me. They were all powerful and they held my life in their hands. The child within me still saw them as gods and to cross them was to cross a deity. When I confronted that lie, the illusion shattered. Not only are my mother and father not God or gods, they don't represent God or his interests. When I stand against my parents, I'm really standing against injustice, abuse and lies. They do not represent anything to do with God and they do not have any power to pronounce judgment on me.

"I want you to know that if you have any plans of writing a book, we will sue you and anyone who has anything to do with it. Your defamation of your father's character will stop. You will not enjoy one penny from any book published about this gross lie."

I thought it was interesting that the threat to sue me was only if I wrote a book. The audience that I'd reached through my website included tens of thousands already. There was plenty of "evidence" of my "slander" and they didn't need to wait for me to write a book. My mother seemed to think the threat could shut me up—that her voice still carried the intimidation it had when I was a little girl.

As it happened, two years after my mother sent this letter, my parents did sue me. It took them that long to fulfill their threat. Their case was very weak and we settled it before it went to trial. It was a distressing time, but when it was over, I felt more empowered and validated than ever.

"And I should let you know that we filed some of your inflammatory statements about your father and me, along with your threat against me, with the Mesa Police Dept."

When I first read that, I was a little girl again, terrified of getting in trouble. It was one thing to be sent to my room and another thing to be sent to jail. But what had I done wrong? I've done nothing illegal or wrong. My dad is the criminal, not me. I'm doing something right in telling my story. I'm standing for the truth and making it easier for other abuse survivors to tell their story. I'm helping to make the world a safer place by talking about how dangerous my childhood was.

Though my mom claimed she and my dad reported me to the police, I don't know if that's really true. There's one thing I have to keep reminding myself: Abusers lie. They will say anything to preserve themselves, which means maintaining their position of power. They justify all kinds of behavior to preserve their advantage.

One of the biggest things that stands out to me about this letter is that it's written by my mother. In fact, this is one of three letters I received from my mother since our "divorce". In the years that I've spoken publicly about my abuse, it's been my mother who's been the one to deny it. My father never made any effort to clear up any "misunderstanding" or to ask me why I'd "lie" about him.

My mother claimed to speak for both of them, but my father was silent. I can only conclude that he didn't want to face me because he knew I'd never be manipulated into silence again. His feigned protests to other people were an attempt to manipulate them, not me.

This threatening letter was a turning point in my recovery process. Seeing how much my parents discounted me stirred something in me. I was determined not to discount myself in the same way. A few days after receiving it, I realized that I hadn't really been standing up for myself enough and decided to report my dad to the police. All along, I'd eliminated the option of reporting him because I reasoned that he probably wasn't hurting anyone anymore. But he had hurt *me*. What he did to me was illegal. It counted.

After that, I was more motivated than ever to stand up for the truth. My parents did their worst but they couldn't shut me up.

I Felt Like Telling was Abusive

Though I'd already confronted many of those fears and false beliefs about telling, like most things in the healing process, there have been many layers to this. Another layer started to surface in the year before my parents sued me for talking about my abuse.

I'd heard reports of my dad's deteriorating body and mind. Though I felt sorry for him, his vulnerable position also angered me. My feelings confused me, but as I examined them, I discovered the source: I believed that I had to stop talking about my abuse now that my dad was in a weakened condition. Because my father was no longer physically, emotionally or mentally stronger than me, I feared that I was taking advantage of someone who couldn't defend himself.

I was afraid that by talking about the things he did to me, I was discounting his personhood in the same way he'd done to me. I feared being abusive.

My mother has said of me:

> *"She has always longed for attention and recognition and the negative recognition is so satisfying to her."*
> *"I regret to say that we raised her to be self-centered and spoiled."*
> *"She is also without scruples, vicious, extreme and without boundaries or a conscience."*

It's clear to me that my mother believes I've been wicked from a very young age and that, though they did their best to instill goodness into me, they were overpowered by the evil in me and by my strong will.

My parents groomed me to accept an identity that made life easier for them—to protect my parents' feelings and reputation and to be ignorant of my value so I wouldn't complain or protest.

As I examined what abuse really is, I realized that telling my story isn't abusive. Hurting someone's feelings isn't the same as abuse. Abuse is about powering over someone else. I'm not taking away my dad's power; I'm claiming my own power. I'm exercising *my* right to tell *my* story of *my* life.

As I faced the truth about my value and identity, I also recognized more universal truths. I didn't cause my parents' emotional distress. My parents' distress came from their own issues. To ask me to carry that responsibility for them was dysfunctional. To have expected that of me as a child was wrong.

I don't have the power to make them feel bad or good, though as a child, I believed that I had that power. I worked hard to make them happy in the hope of being loved. But that was a fantasy that I'm not living in anymore.

My silence wasn't good for anyone—even for my abusers. Those types of secrets are destructive to everyone who keeps them. Truth doesn't destroy people or families; lies do. For incest to occur in a family, it takes more than just an abuser and a victim. It's part of an entire dysfunctional system.

Exposing my abuse gave the entire family an opportunity to heal and to learn more healthy and functional ways to relate to each other. It was their choice to continue to live in the lies, but that doesn't mean they were harmed by the opportunity for another way to live.

Telling the Truth

There is a very strong resistance to disclosing abuse. Keeping the secret was necessary for survival as a child and it's hard to accept that our life no longer depends on our silence. Some of the resistance to talking about our abuse comes from the same reasons that kept us from telling in childhood:

- I thought I was to blame.
- I thought I somehow asked for it.
- I thought I wanted it.
- I confused the sexual abuse for love.
- I was afraid of being blamed.
- I was afraid of not being believed.
- I was afraid of being told that I'm a trouble maker.
- I don't trust myself to know what I experienced. Maybe I made it up or mis-understood what was going on.

Suggested writing:

Did you tell anyone as a child? If so, what kind of a response did you get?

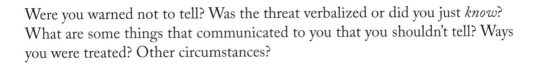

Connecting With Others: Overcoming the Fear of Telling

Were you warned not to tell? Was the threat verbalized or did you just *know*? What are some things that communicated to you that you shouldn't tell? Ways you were treated? Other circumstances?

If you didn't feel safe telling, how did you sense that it wasn't safe? What were you afraid of?

The Rescued Soul

How do you feel about not having anyone to tell as a child?

11
Reaching Out for Help: Building a Support System

I've become very comfortable talking about my abuse now, but when I used to talk about my childhood sexual abuse, I heard familiar accusations: "You just want attention," or "Nobody likes a crybaby." As I poured out the same story again and again to my friends, I felt guilty for wasting their time.

I believed that there was a rule that I was allowed to share a bad experience with one or two people at the most and then I had to stop talking about it or I was "just being a victim". Yet I was compelled to keep talking about my childhood even with the internal accusations and the guilt that it caused.

I was warned that thinking and talking about negative experiences didn't serve any purpose—that it would just make me feel worse. But I was already in pain and it wasn't from talking about my abuse. My trauma and the feelings that went with it were locked up inside of me. As I started to see some benefit from talking about my abuse, I started to question the limited talking rule.

Where did I get the idea that attention is bad or selfish? When I wanted someone to hear me, why did the voice in my head say, "You think you're so important, but you're not"?

Throughout my childhood, that message that I'm not important was repeated in many ways. I was emotionally abandoned if I cried or expressed "negative" feelings. My parents ignored my crying, so I coughed instead. My dad would come to my crib and mock my fake cough. His mocking told me that my needs weren't important and added the additional message that I was a liar who exaggerated my needs.

I learned that I wasn't tolerable unless I was happy so I learned to shut up about my needs and my pain. Acting like everything was okay was the way to avoid more pain of rejection from my parents.

As an adult, whenever I talked about the past, I hated myself for exposing my "badness" and "making" people walk away from me. I expected to be abandoned the same way my parents had abandoned me and I learned to abandon myself during the times that I needed the most comfort.

Seeing where those beliefs and behaviors came from allowed me to see that I'm a worthy of love even when I express my pain or talk about the awful things that happened to me. I used to feel the pressure to stuff my pain or to get it all out quickly. Now I'm patient with myself and no matter how long I talk or grieve, I don't abandon myself in the process. I know I'm worth all the time it takes to heal.

I didn't become so supportive of myself on my own. Throughout my healing journey, I've surrounded myself with loving people who listened to me pour out my heart.

Creating a support circle for myself didn't come naturally. After a lifetime of being the giver in most relationships because of how unworthy I felt, I had many relationships where I didn't get much in return.

During the early days of my healing, the process was completely exhausting. I couldn't afford anything in my life that competed with my healing. Eliminating friends who didn't contribute to my growth was just as important as cultivating supportive friends.

I took inventory of all my relationships—friends, acquaintances, co-workers, family and anyone I had contact with on a regular basis. I evaluated my feelings about each relationship (not each person—for a lot of them, I really enjoyed the person but the relationship didn't make me feel good).

I asked myself three questions:

- How do I feel about myself when I'm with this person?
- Do I feel more or less energy with this person?
- Am I more optimistic or pessimistic about my healing journey with this person?

Feeling inadequate or other negative self-esteem issues around someone doesn't mean they are responsible. Neither does my low energy level or pessimism about my healing. I can take responsibility for my feelings when I'm with someone yet still protect myself from the negative effects.

At the time, it was too much for me to explore all the reasons I felt used in many of my relationships (I saved that for after I healed in other areas) but I was able to begin pulling back from relationships that drained me.

I also starting talking about things I wanted to talk about more with the people who were left. I wasn't ready to ask directly for support yet, but it was my way of testing the relationship to see how eager or resistant they were to meeting my needs.

Slowly, I talked to friends about my abuse and my intention to work on my healing. Their responses told me if they might be willing to be a part of my healing support.

It was difficult for me to ask for the support that I needed. Before I could ask for anyone's help, I needed to define for myself what I was looking for.

Reaching Out for Help: Building a Support System

Making a list was validating to me. After a lifetime of taking care of everyone else, I was out of touch with much of what I wanted and needed. I wasn't accustomed to identifying my needs, much less asking someone for help with them.

I needed to share my needs in a way that fit me and my relationships. Once I made my list, I shared it with the most supportive person in my life—my husband. It was a relief for both of us to have the list. He appreciated knowing what I wanted and didn't want.

For the others who were willing to lend me support, I didn't feel comfortable giving them a list. That felt like I was making demands, not requests. For them, I shared several things on my list that were relevant as they came up organically.

The list of ways I wanted to be supported:

- Let me speak as much or as little as I feel comfortable with. Do not press for details and don't try to change the subject until I'm ready to move on.
- Don't invalidate my experience by sharing something from your own life that you think is similar. You may think you are communicating that you understand my pain, but don't tell me you know exactly how I feel. Please listen to how I'm *telling* you I feel.
- Please don't question my experience. Assure me that you believe me and avoid questions like, "Are you sure?" Even if you know my abusers and view them as a good people, "good people" can do bad things.
- I'm asking you for support. Please don't expect me to take care of your emotions that come out of this discovery. You are entitled to feel however you feel, but don't say things like, "You don't know how much this hurts me." If you aren't able to offer me understanding care at this time, that's fine. But don't turn this around to make it about you.
- Ask me what physical contact I would like. After being violated by touch, sometimes I feel repulsed by touch, especially while my violation is so fresh in my mind. On the other hand, sometimes I do appreciate physical contact that truly is loving and doesn't come with any obligations.
- Don't tell me how I should feel about my perpetrators. That's up to me to sort out for myself. My emotions are complicated. Some days I love my dad and some days I hate him.
- Don't threaten to kill, injure, or otherwise harm my abusers. I have enough emotions to unravel without adding guilt over your actions. I understand that you may feel the need to do something to "fix" this for me. Please know that if you harm my abuser, that is not for me. That is for you. If you really want to honor my feelings, don't complicate my healing process. I don't need the added burden of worrying about you or my abusers.

- Don't confuse who I am with the things that happened to me. Sexual abuse carries so much shame and I already feel different from others. Be sensitive to my wounded places, but don't view me as defective. I'm still the same person you knew before I told you about my abuse.
- Don't try to control how I deal with this. It's my decision if I want to see a therapist or contact the police. I've already lost control through the abuse and I need to regain it by healing in my own way and at my own pace.
- My emotions may appear to be a roller coaster at times. There may be sadness one day, anger the next and avoidance after that. Do not assume that because I'm not crying that I'm not bothered by the abuse or that I'm over it. Crying was considered a weakness in my family and sometimes I feel too vulnerable to show my emotions. Sometimes, I don't even feel any emotions, but that doesn't mean I'm ready to move on.
- Educate yourself so you know what to expect. Do your own research on sexual abuse, the results and the healing process.
- Don't ask how long my healing process will take. I don't know. If it were up to me, I wouldn't have to do this. But I do.
- I experienced a loss and need to be allowed to grieve. Allow me to grieve without trying to fix me. Don't try to make me laugh when I'm sad. You may feel more comfortable with laughter than with tears, but that's not what I need.
- Don't say, "Just forgive him and let it go." Or "Why try to dig up the past?" I'm not trying to dig up the past just for your sympathy or attention. Abuse can have serious consequences if it is not thoroughly dealt with. Believe me, I've tried to forget this and I can't. I need to face the pain so I can leave it there and move toward a better future.

Suggested writing:

Do you have a support system in place? Is there anything standing in the way of gathering more support for yourself?

Reaching Out for Help: Building a Support System

Do you feel comfortable asking for help? If not, what does it mean to you to ask for help?

If I ask for help, it means....

If I ask for help, I feel....

Do you hear any internal accusations if you ask for your needs to be met? What are the voices saying to you? Do those voices sound familiar? Do you remember anyone else communicating that to you—either verbally or through their actions?

When you've asked for help before, what happened when your request was honored? What happened when it wasn't? What meaning did you draw from it? How did you feel?

Make a list of some concrete things you need in order to feel supported.

Sources of support:

- Talking to your partner or significant other
- Talking to friends
- Participating in a support group—face-to-face or online
- Talking to a therapist

www.OvercomingSexualAbuse.com is my website, which is an excellent resource for online support.

12
Owning My Power: Overcoming Victim Mentality

The first sexual abuse I remember was from when I was about one year old. My grandma was watching me while my parents went to Jamaica. Unfortunately, she wasn't watching me very well. My uncle found me alone and took me someplace private. He took off my pants and diaper and started touching me.

He was rough with me and I fought to get away. Frustrated by my kicking and squirming, my uncle squeezed my legs and pressed me against whatever surface I was on. Discomfort turned to pain and I learned the price of resistance.

I was a victim.

"Victim" is a label that is used with distain and disgust by those inside and outside the survivor community. Among other things, it's come to mean someone who is needy, negative, addicted to drama and attention-seeking. I used to prefer being called a whore rather than a victim.

This unjust perception of a victim serves abusers and abusive systems. Judging victims is part of victim blaming. It's communicated in various ways:

- "You deserve what you tolerate."
- "You create your own reality."
- "You must have wanted it since you didn't report it."
- "You should have been more careful."
- "You must have done something to provoke it."
- "Fool me once, shame on you; fool me twice, shame on me."
- "It takes two to tango."

In reality, being a victim is falling under the power of someone or something else. It's a lack of power. The powerlessness might result from being smaller, weaker, younger, slower, less knowledgeable, less experienced, having less authority, or having less social status. At the heart of victimization is the fact that victims are overcome by a greater power.

Victim Blaming

I blamed myself for my abuse as a way to survive my childhood. Blaming myself gave me the sense of control I needed—that I was desperate for. To accept that I was helpless, that there was nothing I could have done, felt like death. However, if there was something wrong with me then I could work to fix it so there was hope of better treatment.

As an adult, going from one abusive relationship to another seemed to confirm that I was to blame for my abuse and that I had always been to blame—even in childhood. I was the common denominator. Some people who saw my cycle of abusive relationships that followed me into adulthood judged me for "allowing" it. I deserved whatever I had coming to me.

Supposedly, the remedy to "being a victim" was to accept the blame so I could make the necessary changes.

Does that mean that if I didn't break something, I can't fix it? If I didn't make the mess, I can't clean it up? I'm a mother so I know that's certainly not true! But I tried for years to apply that to my abuse. I had to accept "my part" in it so I could move forward.

In my healing, I've found that freedom coincides with the truth. If it's not true, it may help me to cope for a time, but it won't set me free. It won't lead to empowering choices and actions. It won't promote love for myself or others—only dysfunction.

The truth is that victims don't make abusers victimize them. To believe that is to say that perpetrators are the true victims—their choice was dictated by the victim. If the victim hadn't mouthed off, if the victim had worn more clothes, if the victim hadn't been walking home alone, the abuser wouldn't have been "forced" to violate them.

That was the way I thought when I was married to my abusive husband. I believed that I provoked him to abuse me. Unconsciously, I knew the cycle of abuse—the build-up, the explosion, the honeymoon. The build-up was agonizing. I knew the explosion was coming, but when??? I had to get it over with and get to the honeymoon part of the cycle, which is what I lived for. The only choice I thought I had was when I'd be abused—not if.

In reality, my ex-husband was looking for any excuse to belittle me and to take away more freedom. He was waiting to twist something I said or did into a reason to punish me.

Abusers justify their punishment by finding a so-called weakness. The weakness doesn't even have to make sense. The flaw or mistake could be "too fat" or "too skinny", "too pretty" or "too ugly", "too stupid" or "a know-it-all". What's ideal one day is a mistake the next. The standards change to keep the victim insecure and self-doubting.

Owning My Power: Overcoming Victim Mentality

I've lived under the control of many abusers and each one considered different qualities a weakness.

I deserve to be treated respectfully, no matter what flaws I have—or I'm thought to have. The truth is that I'm not responsible for my abuser's behavior.

Accepting blame is only helpful if I really am at fault. If I keep getting fired from every job because I'm constantly late, blaming my boss for unfair standards won't help me; blaming traffic won't help me. I'll have employment problems until I recognize my responsibility and do something to change my behavior.

Accepting responsibility for things that *are* my fault can be the first step to improving my life, but accepting responsibility for things that are *not* my fault can also keep me in the cycle of abuse and failure.

One of the problems with accepting false blame is that I became even more angry with myself. I was caught in a game I could never win. That didn't empower me to change the circumstances or myself. If I was somehow responsible for my abuse, what good would it do to leave my abuser? If I deserved the abuse, why should I fight it?

I needed to see who truly deserved the blame.

The truth is that I can place the responsibility on the perpetrators of my abuse while still taking responsibility for picking up the pieces of my life. I can acknowledge it was the abuser's fault and still have power to heal.

Victim Mentality

When my uncle abused me, my instinct was to resist him. When I tried to oppose him, instead of helping, it only hurt me more.

From that and other abuses, I learned to yield, to be nice, to be quiet. Compliance was my defense against increased harm. While I was a child being victimized, that behavior served me.

I remember visiting my grandma again when I was around eleven years old. The same uncle was there and I recall talking with him and standing in a seductive pose. It was my way of telling him, "I won't resist whatever you do to me. Just don't hurt me."

As an adult, I continued to believe that safety came from being agreeable. That was victim mentality. Victim mentality is the belief that I don't have any choice about my decisions or actions. Victim thinking is remaining in survival mode. It's the failure to recognize my own power. It's failing to see that though I *was* helpless, I'm not anymore.

It felt life-threatening to give up blaming myself for the abuse. I resisted seeing myself as a victim, but recognizing that I had no control over my circumstances or my abusers was one of the first steps in owning my power. It was the exchange of the illusion of power for real power. It's ironic that to get my power back, I had to acknowledge how powerless I had been.

Owning My Power

I've realized a little at a time over many years that I really am capable of improving my own life in big and small ways. As a childhood victim, one of my only powers was complaining. As I've transitioned into viewing myself as an empowered adult, I've learned to listen to my thoughts. I've become alert to grumbling or whiny expressions that are meant to gain me sympathy—as though I'm completely at someone else's mercy.

When I was still learning to own my power, I planned to complain to my husband that he never spent any time with me, but I stopped myself. That sounded like an accusation, not the invitation that I intended. I was blaming him and placing all the responsibility for our relationship on him, as though I was powerless. In the past, whining didn't accomplish anything other than drawing us further apart, which was the opposite effect I wanted.

This time, as an empowered person, I said to my husband, "We haven't spent much time together lately and I miss you. Are you free for dinner on Thursday?" I took responsibility for my feelings and my relationship and I had a date.

I've also learned to listen to my anger. I often feel angry when I feel overpowered or controlled. My past taught me that I don't have any choice in being overpowered and it's been a process of teaching myself that I do.

On one occasion, I made plans with a friend to see a movie. She planned to pick me up at 3pm, but phoned at 1:30pm to say she was an hour ahead of schedule and that she'd pick me up in 30 minutes. She thought it would be fun to go shopping first. When she called, I was just making lunch and her schedule change meant I wouldn't have time to eat before she arrived. I had something planned right after my outing with her, so lunch was my last chance to eat until the end of the day.

After we hung up I got angry. In my mind, my friend was keeping me from eating. I felt like I didn't have a choice.

I challenged that thought. Did I have a choice? I realized I wasn't being forced to follow her plan so I examined my options. I could eat first while she waited for me or I could just cancel if she didn't want to wait. Once I realized that I had options and decided what to do, my anger went away. I was empowered.

I was conditioned to believe I didn't have any choices. I was a victim in childhood but I'm not a victim anymore. Now, I think in terms of what options I do have rather than what options I don't have. Victim mentality kept me from making empowered decisions but now I own my power to improve my life.

Owning My Power: Overcoming Victim Mentality

Suggested writing:

If someone calls you a victim of abuse, how do you feel about that?

How does it feel to say that you didn't have any control over what happened to you?

Consider how few things you actually had control over when you were a child. What decisions were made for you?

Finish this sentence:
I'm not to blame for my abuse because...

Can you identify situations or relationships you're in now where you feel a lack of power? Can you think of ways you actually *are* empowered to improve things you don't like?

13
Embracing My Anger

After my uncle sexually and physically abused me at my grandmother's house, there was a change in me. When my parents returned from Jamaica, they noticed that I was angry and concluded that I was mad at my mother for leaving me. They treated my anger like a big joke and continued to chuckle about it for years.

My anger was discounted, but none of us could ignore my dad's anger. We tiptoed around him when he was unhappy for fear of setting off one of his flights of fury. I had the sense that we were all anger's prisoners, even my dad. He seemed to be controlled by it too.

I survived by denying my anger and complying, but occasionally, my true feelings leaked out. When I was seven, my parents sent me to my room for something I thought was unjust. I felt like I would explode. I reacted by punching my bedroom window. The drapes were lined and the window was covered in protective film, so the glass broke but didn't shatter.

I don't know what terrified me more, how out of control I felt—I was just a little girl, but the energy that came out of me made me feel fierce—or my parents' angry reaction. I didn't want the consequences of expressing anger again.

The anger didn't disappear. It was buried, but it was buried alive. It scratched and clawed and cried out, mostly through abusive acts toward myself. As I got older, I also occasionally blew up at people close to me. I didn't relate it to my abuse; I considered it another of my personality flaws that I was born with.

As I started to take an honest look at my past, anger seemed to bubble out of me. Even minor boundary violations triggered a much stronger reaction than what seemed appropriate. I had trouble being in public for fear of seriously hurting someone.

I was reacting to all the times that my boundaries were violated in the past when I was either not allowed to object to in childhood or when I *believed* that I wasn't allowed to object to in adulthood.

I wrote this letter to express my anger toward the people I didn't even know:

97

Dear John Q. Public:

EXCUSE YOU!!!! I would like to be able to walk down the street or sit in a public place without you bumping into me as though you don't see me. Are you so inept as to have no control over your elbows, arms or bags? You have enough room to go around, so stop intruding on my frickin space!!!!. I'm tired of making myself smaller so that you don't hit me. YOU make you and your stuff fit into the space allocated for you.

Stop pretending that you don't see me as you approach me on the sidewalk. You expect me to step aside for you as though it's your sidewalk. Do you think life is a parade for you and that everyone should just make way since you're SO important and I'm not? Why do you think that since you're in a hurry, you can insist on going first? You act as though your destination is more important than mine. You don't know who I am, yet you've made a decision about your value compared to mine. I'm SICK OF IT!!!!

Just talking to you like this makes me laugh. I'm hearing myself and I guess I've been blaming you for how I feel. Of course you're just trying to get through the day, the same as I am. Maybe you're in your own little world and aren't thinking of me, but that doesn't mean I have to believe that your treatment of me makes me less important. I've been giving you too much power. I'm important and I don't need you to prove that to me. It's just true.

When I wrote that letter, I heard myself in a way I hadn't before. I thought it would merely help rid me of some anger, but through it, I realized that I believed that the whole world was against me. I took every careless move or bump personally. I connected how others behaved toward me and what I believed about my worth.

The mistreatment was not only a reminder of the abuses of my childhood, it was a trigger of the lies I believed. In every careless intrusion I heard, "You're nothing and I can do whatever I want to you."

Around that time, I was preparing a meal but the food package was already opened on the bottom. I as I picked it up, it slipped out on the floor. I felt robbed. I picked it up and slammed it across the kitchen. I watched with satisfaction as it slid down the wall, leaving a mess behind it. It was a dramatic moment that couldn't be ignored, which was the opposite of the invisible feeling I had as a child. It was my expression, "I WANT TO BE SEEN!"

I also had a persistent fantasy of stabbing my mother in the face. The recurring image of something so horrific was quite disturbing. I'd never consider doing anything like that; blood makes me nauseous and even hurting someone's feelings bothers me.

Embracing My Anger

I tried to suppress my feelings by thinking loving thoughts and imagining kind things about my mother. I berated myself. I distracted myself. But the frequency and intensity of those thoughts wouldn't allow me to discount them.

I had to own my desires and find out their source. Where did they come from? What purpose did they serve? What was the significance of destroying my mother's face? The fantasy was an important clue.

I remembered an incident from my childhood. I was alone with my dad in my parent's bedroom. My mom took great care in decorating the whole house, but especially their room. The bedding matched the drapes, which coordinated with the carpet. Their bed rested on a raised platform that was designed to make it the focal point of the room.

My dad perched me on the edge of the platform while he sat on the floor across from me. He had several pornographic magazines spread out next to him. While my dad put his finger inside of me, I looked up at the drapes and thought that appearances were all that mattered to my mom. She could make the house look like a palace, but it would always be a dungeon.

My mom was more interested in image than reality. I was enraged that she chose to sacrifice me so she could keep our family looking perfect. My slashing fantasy was an expression of my anger over her effort to make everything *look* nice, rather than actually making it nice. Her face represented the image that was so important to her.

One of the primary ways I expressed my feelings toward my mother was by letter writing. I wrote many letters and emails to her. This is one of them:

Dear Mom,

You're such a LIAR!!!! You claim I'm the one who's lying and you hide behind your religious façade and your pretty house and pretty clothes. You're disgusting! With all the effort you put into pretending you're so good, you could have actually been a good person.

All my life, I thought I was the problem. I thought if my own mother didn't love me, I must be unlovable. I took on all the hatred, resentment, judgments, and disgust that you directed toward me and turned it on myself. I learned to feel those things about me.

I worked so hard for you to love me. All my life, I wanted to be close to you. I worked to get good grades, I tried to behave myself, but you didn't seem to see me.

When I was ten, the school psychologist noticed something wrong with me after she observed me for only a few minutes. YOU LIVED WITH ME!!! WHY DIDN'T YOU NOTICE???????? You never saw me at all.

But I WAS THERE!!!! And my abuse DID happen!!!! No matter how much you deny that and accuse me of living in a fantasy world, your husband did disgusting things to me. YOU were disgusting toward me too!!! How dare you make your life easier by sacrificing me!! I deserved better than that!!!!

My buried anger was coming out. Through my anger, I was not only objecting to the abuse, but its false messages. My anger was the shift into validating myself instead of the lies. It was my declaration that I deserved to be treated better.

Freedom to Be Angry

All my life, I judged myself for being angry. I denied my anger and tried to cover it with more acceptable feelings. I was doing the same thing my mom did—I was decorating over the things I didn't want to see or feel.

As long as I rejected and denied my anger, I didn't control it; it controlled me. It spilled out unintentionally on me and on others I cared about.

Displaced anger is impossible to get rid of. As long as I projected it in all the wrong places, I could never work through it; there was a never-ending supply.

Giving myself permission to "feel what I feel" has proven the shortest way out of that emotion. Processing my anger allowed me to resolve it.

Anger Toward My Primary Abuser

For years after I acknowledged that my dad had sexually abused me, I just didn't feel very angry toward him. As I learned, there are many reasons survivors don't direct their anger toward their primary abusers:

- It feels too threatening to oppose someone in a position of power or that I view as powerful.
- The belief that the abuse was my fault so the only one to be angry with was me.
- My dad was someone I loved. He was my only source of affection and attention when I was a child. I was afraid to unleash anger for fear of losing a relationship with him.
- I was so enmeshed with my dad that loyalty to him was loyalty to myself. (One of the ways I broke that bond of loyalty was by telling the secret. The secret was something only we shared, which was a perverted form of intimacy. Breaking the secret broke that hold.)
- The abuse taught me that I'm not valuable so anyone is entitled to treat me however they want to. The abuse is justified.
- I felt sorry for my dad because he had such a hard life.
- I was afraid of judging him because I know I'm not a perfect parent.

- My dad did so many nice things too, so it was hard to comprehend that he could do such bad things.
- I was afraid that I'd become an abuser like my dad.
- Getting angry felt like the end of our relationship—that I was giving up hope that he'd ever love me.

Identifying my fears helped me face them. As I faced my fears, I felt ready to write this to my dad:

Dear Dad,

The healthier I get, the clearer I see the real you. I used to make excuses for you by reminding myself how bad your own childhood was. I told myself that I'm not a perfect parent, so I shouldn't judge. I covered up your rape of my childhood by thinking about the magic shows you did and the family vacations you took us on. I told myself that you did the best you could.

But you didn't do your best, did you? There was nothing "best" about forcing me into sex with you or with your friends. I can't pretend anymore.

One of the worst ways you hurt me was the way you treated me like a sick freak when I started doing the things I learned from you. You passed me around to other men—did you really think I wouldn't learn to pass myself around? You judged me for doing that, yet you seemed to think it was okay for you to do that. Why was it right that you treated me like a prostitute, but it was wrong for me to treat myself like one? Were you really that shocked or were you distancing yourself from me to avoid any blame? I remember you and Mom sitting across from me in the living room, just shaking your heads. The unspoken question, even in my own mind, seemed to be, "How could a person end up so bad when they came from such a good family?" I felt so completely alone. And shameful.

You acted like nobody would want me and I believed you. The one thing I wanted was love and connection, but the shame you put on me, the shame that belonged to you, made me think I had forfeited love. You denied me any sense of belonging and then convinced me I would never find it anywhere else either.

In spite of what you did to me, I still wanted a relationship with you. Even though we never talked about the past, I assumed that you regretted it. I thought you had changed and were sorry. And then you attacked again. You attacked Bethany for reporting her father for raping her. You defended the man who was supposed to defend and protect her from the very things he did to her. And for the things you did to me. You haven't changed. Otherwise, you would have recognized the horror of what was done to my daughter, and wouldn't have minimized and excused it. If you had changed, you would have been Bethany's biggest ally, instead of her abuser's ally.

You suck at being a man. In fact, you suck at being a human being. Nearly everyone else who hears about what David did is sickened, yet you don't flinch. You are her grandfather. You sick bastard! I haven't gotten angry with you for what you did to me until now. The way you betrayed Bethany disgusts me and arouses rage toward you, both for what you are doing to her and what you did to me. I hate sharing the same planet with you.

You treated me like an object put on the earth for your own sexual pleasure. You acted as though that was my only value. You laughed with your friends as you told them I would make a good call girl. Then you rented me out. What kind of a father does that? I'm still trying to understand how you can do something so cruel and vile to me, yet act so good to everyone else.

I hate how I learned to think of myself as a result of your image of me. I didn't think I was good for anything except as a sexual toy. I never dared to dream about doing anything important because I was too busy with the nightmare that I'd end up as a prostitute. That was what you made me, but THAT IS NOT WHO I AM!! Do you hear me? I know that now. I was made for much better things than for yours, or anyone else's, pleasure. Finally, I know that. I'm beginning to dream now. I'm going to have a future that is dictated by my own desires, not by fears inspired by you. I will not be controlled by what you did to me or what you said about me. I know those were lies and I don't believe them anymore.

Who are you to dictate my future? I used to see you as so powerful, but now I see that you are the weakest of humans, ruled by your lusts. You traded your masculinity for the degradation of yourself and others. You are not strong. You couldn't even protect your daughter from yourself. You are not a man. A real man would give his child security and instead of making her afraid of you.

I don't want to know you anymore since you remain a sexual predator. I will take the good things that you imparted to me and leave the rest behind.

I started to write the letter from my head, but as I progressed, my heart spoke. Through the words, I poured out all the emotions I didn't know I had. The more I wrote, the more rage rose up. I imagined the hatred flowing up from within me and down my arms and hands and onto the paper. After that, the paper contained more of my anger and pain so I didn't have to carry it.

The Purpose of Anger

The lessons of my childhood taught me that anger leads to pain. Anger meant rejection; it was abusive and out of control. It was emotionally and physically violent.

Embracing My Anger

But that isn't the truth. Anger is only a feeling and it can be directed in ways that are constructive rather than destructive. Merely having an emotion isn't abusive.

Anger is the healthy response to innocent children being abused or about other injustices. It's meant to motivate us to action. It's a signal to protect others or ourselves from harm. The purpose of anger isn't to annihilate life; it's a tool to preserve life.

It's appropriate to feel anger toward the people who didn't protect you, didn't notice you, didn't believe you, blamed you, defended the abuser, told you to forgive or move on, or who didn't show you compassion.

Expressing Anger

The best way to express anger depends on the purpose of the anger. What is the anger saying? What was happening when I became angry? What do I believe about the situation? What am I afraid of? Being taken advantage of? Being violated? Being humiliated? Devalued? There is always an underlying feeling and message that I need to pay attention to.

When I need a physical release, I beat my pillow or scream into it. Other people go running or do some other strenuous activity. I feel a lot clearer headed once I let it out and it's easier to sort out what I need to do then.

In some cases, it's enough to validate my feelings and to release it. But other times, the situation calls for more action. I ask myself how I can use my anger to improve the situation. What is my anger trying to teach me? Sometimes, I need to decide to take better care of myself. I might need to ask for my needs to be met. I might need to confront someone. I might need to adjust my boundaries or my schedule.

Sometimes current situations trigger a much stronger reaction than what the situation really calls for. Usually, it's unprocessed anger from the past that is multiplying its intensity. Even if my anger isn't "justified" by the current situation, I don't judge myself for having a feeling. I look at my feelings as clues to what's going on inside of me and use it for my benefit. I ask myself questions. When have I felt this way before? What does this situation remind me of? When I find myself overreacting to my current circumstance, it's an opportunity to heal from the past.

Benefits of Anger
- Anger helped me transition into compassion for myself.
- Anger helped me to shift from compliance to standing up for myself.
- Anger helped me to take the shame and guilt off of me.

- Anger released me from the compulsion to punish myself through self-harm, self-neglect or self-sabotage.
- Releasing anger released the tension in my body.
- Expressing my anger released mental and emotional tension; I became freer and lighter.
- Owning my anger helped me become more assertive; I didn't feel like I was standing in a position of guilt or inferiority.
- Anger helped me maintain my boundaries and protect myself from more harm.
- Becoming skilled in expressing anger eased my relationships with the people close to me.

Anger is an important part of healing. When it's recognized as a protective energy, and expressed in a healthy way, it's transformed from a pain causing tool to a pain-relieving tool.

Suggested writing:

When someone says to you, "You're angry", how do you feel about that?

If you're having trouble getting angry, try this writing exercise. Finish this sentence:

I don't want to release my anger because....

Embracing My Anger

Write letters to your primary abuser and to each of your parents if they weren't the perpetrators of your abuse. These letters are for you so you don't have to send them. Confront them about the things they did to you or the ways they neglected you. Tell them how the abuse and neglect affected you and how you feel about that.

The Rescued Soul

Embracing My Anger

107

The Rescued Soul

14
Restoring My Boundaries

I don't remember ever feeling safe when I was a child. I was continually vulnerable to my dad's sexual advances. I preferred small, enclosed places like blanket forts or my bedroom closet but when my dad wanted me, he found me.

Part of my self-care now is being very intentional about creating safe spaces in my life. I've designed cozy spots in my home that are beautiful and nurturing, but one of the most important spaces I've reserved for myself is the space of time.

I schedule time just for myself when I'm not available by phone, text, email or any other means. Nobody has unlimited access to me now—not even my husband, not my children, not my best friends. I never had sanctuary as a child, but I'm my own sanctuary now.

For most of my life, I didn't know I had the right to set aside space for myself. I'd spent most of my life at anyone's beck and call. They summoned with a need and I was there.

A funny thing happened when my memories surfaced and I was thrust into the crisis stage of healing. I suddenly couldn't answer my phone. I'd hear it ring and have a strong urge to run away from it. I was anxious just thinking about listening to the messages that were piling up.

I felt silly for having such a strange reaction. I couldn't understand what was going on with me. I considered what I felt: threatened, suffocated, caged, buried. But what could feel so threatening about my phone ringing?

It slowly occurred to me that phone calls meant people in need. After coping so long by taking care of others instead of myself, I cultivated many relationships where I was the giver without receiving much in return. When my focus shifted to my healing, my new thoughts and old feelings exhausted me. I didn't have the energy to care for anyone else. Without being able to verbalize my "no" yet, I was saying no through avoidance and hiding. It was my adult version of building forts or tucking away in my closet.

The abuse violated my boundaries. My body and soul were invaded without regard for my will or my feelings. No one saw me, who I am, what I wanted, what I felt, what I thought. My abusers stole my "no". Anyone could lay claim to my time, energy, body or possessions.

Even if I'd had permission to say no, I feared the consequences. I was criticized for being such a people-pleaser but my well-being depended on making everyone happy when I was a child. My compliance and good behavior were attempts to manipulate my abusers into treating me better. People asked, "Why do you care so much about what people think?" I was conditioned to care. Controlling people's attitudes about me was survival.

My Revolt Against Control

Not surprisingly, my biggest boundary issues were with my parents. Revolting against their abuse and control started by accident. I didn't intend to assert myself. Actually, when I stood up to them, it was in defense of my husband's boundaries. I didn't feel so strongly about protecting my own yet.

My husband had written about the abusive practices of the former church we attended, where he and my parents were part of the pastoring staff. We'd since broken off our relationship with that church but my parents were still very much involved.

The senior pastors sent my mother to silence my husband. She tried to guilt me into convincing Don to retract his statements. She claimed her job was in jeopardy because of our stand against the senior pastor's behavior. We knew from a past instance that those threats were a tactic they used to "get people under control."

When I challenged my mother on her manipulation, I told her that I'd been hurt by the many lies she'd told me in the past to control me. I told her that I wanted a closer and healthier relationship with her but that I couldn't get closer to her with the lies between us.

I thought if my mom understood, she would accept my husband's right to continue writing and would stop lying in order to protect her relationship with me.

How wrong I was! My mother was furious. Setting boundaries seemed to be viewed as hostile aggression. She seemed to believe that I was denying her something that belonged to her if I resisted. I was a resource to be exploited for her personal use. I was property that didn't have any rights over my thoughts, feelings, beliefs or values. How dare I think for myself! How dare I not comply!

My mother's control and manipulation tactics escalated. When none of them succeeded, both of my parents walked out of my life. My dad's words to me were, "We're not allowed to talk to you or know you."

On an unconscious level, that's what I feared and worked to avoid all my life. "If you don't do everything we want, we'll leave you." Abandonment was the price to pay for not conforming. No wonder I'd conformed for so long.

Restoring My Boundaries

Accepting My Abusers' Boundaries

To avoid abandonment, I'd accepted the responsibility for my entire relationship with my parents. If there was something that needed to be repaired, I needed to do it. After they left, for the first time in my life, I had to accept that I was powerless to convince them to love me or to treat me better. I needed to accept my parents' right to think for themselves and decide their own priorities. I needed to respect their right to discontinue their relationship with me. I needed to accept their no:

"No, we won't admit we did anything harmful to you."
"No, we won't apologize."
"No, we won't choose to have a relationship with you if you don't submit to us."

My parents may not behave, think, or feel the way I want them to, but they are free to make their own choices.

Taking Responsibility for My Boundaries

To focus on other people's boundaries—their behavior, their responsibilities, their choices, their beliefs, their opinions, their feelings, their attitudes, their values—is to assume responsibility for them. While I was occupied with trying to placate my parents or mend things with them, I was abandoning my own boundaries. I'd already lost so much of myself to the abuse. I needed to accept my parents' right to reject me, which helped to shift my focus onto me.

I deserved my own time and attention and slowly learned to provide that. I had to own my own feelings and opinions. Right or wrong, they are mine and I don't need anyone's permission to think or feel them. I learned to be firm in my own no:

"No, I won't stay silent about the abuse."
"No, I'm not going to protect your reputation at my expense."
"No, I'm not going to continue to submit to your abuse."
"No, I won't settle for a one-sided relationship."
"No, I don't agree with you."

Five years after my parents walked out of my life, they filed a lawsuit against me for defamation of character and intentional infliction of emotional distress. They demanded that I stop talking about my father sexually abusing me.

By that time, I was secure in my boundaries. I didn't take responsibility for my parents' feelings. I didn't care that they weren't happy with me. I knew I had a right to tell my story of my life. I was determined to stand up for myself.

Their betrayal was unbelievably painful, but I survived. My parents' displeasure didn't kill me. Their rejection didn't harm me. I don't have to go along with things I don't like and I don't have to be quiet.

Setting Boundaries Isn't Punishment

The way my parents exercised their boundaries was done in a punishing and threatening way. There was no verbal, "Submit to us OR ELSE!" but the threat of abandonment was communicated through the way they shamed me and withdrew their approval whenever I displeased them. Their version of boundaries was intended to inspire fear—which it did.

Boundaries aren't for controlling other people. They aren't about powering over someone. Healthy boundaries come from being secure in your own power and knowing that you have choices—but also respecting the other person's power and choices.

"When you do this, I feel this. I'd like to be treated like this. If you continue this, I need to protect myself by doing this."

"When you are late for our appointment, I feel disrespected. I'd like you to be on time and if an emergency comes up, I'd like you to call me instead of keeping me waiting. If you continue to be late, I won't meet with you anymore."

When I communicate a boundary in this way, I'm taking responsibility for my feelings and my desires. I'm stating my intention to make my choice about what to do if I encounter the situation again. I'm taking responsibility for my behavior. This also acknowledges the other person's right to choose their behavior. He's free and I'm free.

When the other person doesn't honor my boundary, I still can. I do that by following through on the action that protects me and my interests. If he doesn't respect my time, I respect it by protecting it from him.

If the other person continues to dishonor my boundaries, I move the boundaries out further. Sometimes, that means leaving the relationship.

The way my parents used boundaries didn't respect my right to think, feel and act according to my convictions. My husband and I weren't harming them to express our opinions. It may have hurt their feelings that I didn't agree with them, but that's not abusive. It didn't take away their power.

Maintaining my boundaries is ongoing. I don't encounter many people in my life who dishonor them. People started respecting my boundaries when I started believing that I had a right to set those limits—when I truly believed that I was worth protecting and that it was my responsibility to do the protecting.

Restoring My Boundaries

Abuse demolished my boundaries and I didn't have any sense of control over my environment. In my present life, feeling safe doesn't come from trusting or knowing how others will behave; it comes from trusting myself to respond accordingly. Being secure in my boundaries allows me to feel safe in my world.

Suggested writing:

If you have trouble saying no, finish this sentence:
If I say no…

Is there something in your life right now that you feel a particular need to protect by saying no? What is happening?

Do you trust in your ability to create a safe space for yourself? If not, what limits can you establish to feel safe? What are some ways for you to take responsibility for protecting your time, energy, body, physical space, and possessions?

Are people in your life comfortable with your limits? How do they respond to the limits you set? If they don't honor your boundaries, what can you do to honor your boundaries?

Are you in relationships that depend on you not to ask for much? How do you decide what "too much" is? Where did you learn that you couldn't ask for too much?

15
Reconciling With My Body

Not too long after my memories started to surface, my husband and I were strolling down the Walk of Fame in Hollywood, which was close to where we lived. The boulevard is filled with locals, tourists, costumed actors, musicians and homeless people. Don knew many of the regulars from his almost daily walks. He knew most of their stories—their histories and their hopes. We'd never get very far without one of them stopping to say hello.

Don had first met Muscles while Muscles was working as a bodyguard, though he had lost his job and become homeless. He was big and tall enough that Don spotted him when we were nearly a half a block away. I'd been hearing about Muscles for a year or more but hadn't yet met him. I extended my hand to him as we approached, but he grabbed my arms and pulled me against him. He put his sweaty face against mine and said to my husband, "What's yours is mine."

I watched it all happen from the streetlight above us. I didn't pull away; I didn't voice my disgust. As soon as the man released me, I ran home without a word.

Throughout my life, I've escaped from the unpleasantness that was happening with my body—dental visits, medical exams, sexual experiences. In fact, even if I didn't "leave" my body, I never really considered myself a resident of my body. I didn't identify with it as mine. It wasn't something I felt responsible for or cared for.

I criticized my body mercilessly. When I looked in the mirror, I'd look away in shame for having to be encased in something so fat and ugly.

As I was emotionally healing from my abuse, I started having health issues. I got mad at my body for letting me down. I felt like it failed me when I was weak or in pain. I'd say things like, "My kidney is giving me trouble again." The truth is I'd given my kidney trouble, not the other way around. I didn't give my body what it needed to thrive and it's done the best it could with what I provided.

My health problems scared me enough that I wanted to reconcile with my body. I needed to be in tune to its signals so I could avoid a total health crisis. I wrote this letter to my body:

Dear Body,

Why the hell can't you cooperate with me??? Am I really asking too much to expect you to be able to work normal hours without breaking down? Do you have to be so difficult???!!! You're weak and you make me sick!

I wish I didn't have to be stuck with you. Why are you so misshapen and FAT? You embarrass me. I wish I didn't have to be seen with you. Do you know who you remind me of? The two worst people I know—my parents. Every time I look in the mirror, I think of THEM. It makes me want to gouge your eyes out. Oh, shit! I'm so sorry! That's really not your fault that you look like them. You may remind me of them on the outside, but that doesn't mean I'm like them. I'm nothing like them. Except I did get my dad's sense of humor and my mom's laugh, but that's okay.

Still, I feel you need to be punished for attracting my dad and the other men who hurt me. If you weren't so small and weak, that never would have happened. Now that I think about it, I'm keeping you weak by not caring for you properly, aren't I?

I guess a lot of the things I've been blaming you for are really my fault. I resented you, so I didn't pay attention to the times you tried to tell me what you needed. I've been expecting you to serve me, but I haven't been serving you.

I remember how my dad watched how much food I gave you. It makes me laugh to remember the horror on his face as he watched me add to your weight. Am I keeping you fat so you aren't small? I hate the way he looks at you when you're thin and I hate the way he looks at you when you're fat. Heck, maybe he's the one who needs his eyes gouged out.

Okay, the answer isn't in him. He can't do anything to me anymore. I hate the way I've treated you because of him. Crap! I've become your abuser too. I've felt the same disgust about your size that he did. That makes me mad that I've been so influenced and controlled by him. I'm sorry for how I've treated you. I didn't see that you were doing the best you could to survive. Me too. I guess we're in this together. I'll do better taking care of you. For all that you've been through, you've held up very well. Thanks for being there for me. I appreciate you and I'll start being there for you.

All my life, I'd judged my body the way my dad and others did. If I saw something about my body that was considered a flaw to others, especially men, I considered it a flaw too. In victim mentality, pleasing others was the way I survived so anything about me that wasn't "pleasing" was my enemy. Through my harsh treatment and neglect, I'd turned on my body just as violently as my abusers had.

Reconciling With My Body

After a lifetime of neglect, I had to retrain myself to pay attention to when I was thirsty, hungry, tired or in pain. In the beginning, I had to be very intentional about paying attention. Every hour, I stopped what I was doing to scan my body for possible needs. Did it need to eat? What was it hungry for? Did I need to rest? Move around? Change my position? Change my activity?

Eventually, I worked out a flexible eating and exercise plan that was empowering. It didn't come naturally to be so attentive but as I cared for my body in practical ways, I felt more connected and responsible for my body. I started to take pride in it for the first time in my life and it became easier to listen to its needs.

I also did an exercise of addressing every part of my body by name. I started with my feet and worked my way up. I considered how the particular parts of my body had been used in my abuse—and, in essence stolen from me. It was like being forced to watch my child being tortured. I let the feelings emerge and let myself grieve. I'd blamed my body for participating and even though it was innocent and didn't need forgiveness, I needed to acknowledge its innocence and ask it to forgive me for abandoning and betraying it.

Loving Touch

My childhood experience of being touched was mostly limited to sexual touch. The sexual touch was harmful, but not being touched in nurturing ways was just as harmful. Loving touch is necessary for human development and health. I needed healing from the abuse *and* the neglect.

As an adult, I never enjoyed being touched other than in sexual ways. Being lovingly caressed or stroked annoyed me. I didn't appreciate hugs. I didn't see the point of any of that.

I thought massages would be a way to become more connected to my body. Every massage has been a different experience—some good and some not so good—but I learned something about myself every time. I started by talking with a massage therapist about my comfort level and where I wanted to be touched and what areas I wanted her to avoid. That might have been the first time I'd ever taken ownership of what I wanted and how I expressed it. That was empowering.

Some massages released body memories and stored emotions. Those were exhausting, but they gave me a sense of relief. During other massages, I dissociated by talking most of the way through instead of focusing on the feeling of being touched. Over time, I've connected to the experience and I even feel pleasure now.

As I've learned to stay present in my pain and to own my power, my body has become a less threatening place to be. Now, I savor the warmth of a shower and the gentleness of my husband's caress. I enjoy having my grandkids cuddled next to me and the embrace of old friends.

Though I separated myself from my body in my mind to survive the abuse, it was only in my *mind*. I really can't separate my body from the rest of me. My body and I are one. As I've connected to my mind and emotions more deeply, I've connected more and more to my body. What affects one affects the other. I'm a whole person, intact, together. I'm with me.

Suggested writing:

Write a letter to your body. What do you feel about it?

Reconciling With My Body

The Rescued Soul

Write to the individual parts of your body. Write about how each part was used in your abuse. Write about how you feel about that. Tell each body part that it was innocent. Ask each part to forgive you for however you've neglected or abused it.

16
Remembering My Past: Memories Journal

My abuse has been denied, minimized, redefined, and discounted.

- My mother claimed it was impossible that my dad abused me and that I'm living in a fantasy world to imagine that.
- As my dad was abusing me, he told me it was love and now denies it ever happened.
- People have told me it was part of making me who I am and that I should be thankful for it because now I can help others.
- Others have told me, "Well at least he didn't physically hurt you."
- My church said it was wrong for me to expose my parents and that I needed to forgive before I would deserve healing.

I learned to deny, minimize, redefine and discount my own abuse too.

- I told myself that the things that happened to me were no big deal and that it wasn't damaging enough to even address.
- I excused my parents' actions by convincing myself they did the best they could and that my dad had a worse childhood than I did.
- I believed that I didn't have a right to complain about anything my parents did and that I should just be grateful that I was born in the first place.

My journal has been my place to set the record straight. The things that were done to me were serious. They really did happen. It wasn't for some higher purpose. It was awful and I didn't deserve it.

My journal is my private space to record the abuse, express my feelings and to sort out the truth from the lies. Sometimes, it was very difficult to note the ugliest parts of my experiences and feelings, but journal writing keeps them contained in a small, designated space instead of freely floating around inside of me. I can access them when I want, but until then, they are tucked away.

I hid the truth from myself by only seeing one childhood incident at a time. I continued to make excuses each time by dismissing the current mistreatment since "they usually treated me well." Collecting my experiences in one place allowed me to see the life-long pattern of mistreatment and the relationship with my parents as a whole.

When I wrote some of my memories, I didn't even believe them as I was writing them. But I committed to recording my flashbacks, recalled memories, recovered memories and my dreams. My journal started to show me the truth I'd been hiding from myself. Seeing how consistent those things were with how I'd always felt helped me to accept them. The pages validated what I was just beginning to validate for myself.

Memories surfaced that made so much sense of my entire life, but how could they be real? I alternated between grasping the truth in relief and pushing it away in fear. Denial gave me a break from facing the truth but the journal helped me to find it again when I was ready.

A lot of my healing journal is about the sexual abuse, but there were all kinds of abuse that I needed to acknowledge and heal. Sexual abuse takes place in the context of other types of abuse: Psychological, emotional, verbal, spiritual and physical abuse. Healing from sexual abuse has meant looking at how I was mistreated in other ways.

Sometimes, it was just too revealing to write out everything. I felt too exposed or crazy or shameful to see them in print. I'd start to write something and wouldn't be able to finish it for days or weeks or months. Sometimes, I'd just write, "baby boy incident" until I felt ready to face more.

Writing reveals truth—the truth that's been buried. It tells the secrets I was commanded to keep.

I've learned to ask myself questions as a way to overcome my own objections and fears. Somehow, I know the answers to the questions. It comes from somewhere inside of me that is waiting to be called upon.

Why do I resist writing about the things that happened to me?
I don't want to write because…

What am I afraid of?
I'm afraid that if I write about my abuse…

I titled the various memories in my healing journal with these headings:

- Dreams & Nightmares
- Recalled Memories
- Recovered Memories
- Flashbacks

Remembering My Past: Memories Journal

Recalled Memories

Some of my recalled memories were of the sexual abuse, though I hadn't recognized them as abusive until I started to heal. Most of my recalled memories were of other types of abuse—emotional, psychological, verbal, and physical. Neglect is also a type of abuse. I recorded events that felt discounting, that seemed strange, or that I had bookmarked—there were many events from my childhood that seemed significant in some way, which is why I remembered them. Until I started writing them down and tying the pieces together, they never made sense. I had "bookmarked" them all those years ago, yet as isolated incidents, I didn't understand their meaning. As I started collecting them in my journal, I saw the pattern of mistreatment and how that falsely informed me of my identity and value.

A few of my recalled memories:

> *In the summer before grade three started, I was in our backyard, running around the pool. I slipped and my right leg went into the pool while the rest of me landed on the cement surface.*
>
> *I ran into the house crying. My paternal grandmother was visiting and asked me what was wrong. I didn't have words for that part of my body that I'd injured. I was embarrassed to be hurt there. I pulled down my pants to show her that I was bleeding. She became impatient with me and walked away.*
>
> *I was still crying and my mother walked into the bathroom. I showed her the blood. The only thing she said was that she didn't think I was starting my period and then she walked away.*

As I journaled about that incident, I had a sense that I wasn't supposed to talk about hurting "down there". I felt like it was my fault and I didn't deserve comfort.

My grandmother and mother were dismissive of my pain. I thought that I'd been seriously hurt so I wasn't only in physical pain, I was also afraid. I felt abandoned. My body and emotions were ignored.

> *When I was a teenager, we had a family meeting around the kitchen table. I told my parents I didn't want to be left alone with my brother. My dad changed the subject. I started pleading with him to listen to me. My dad continued to discount what I was saying, but he suddenly seemed worried. I told him that my brother had been beating me when they weren't home. My dad seemed relieved. He said something dismissive and moved on.*

Thinking back to that time, my dad wasn't interested in my safety. My brother was a year and a half younger than me, but he was bigger and stronger than me by that time. He was brutal when he was mad.

123

I have the feeling that my dad was worried that I was going to tell them that my brother had raped me. I don't think my father's relief was from learning that my brother was "only" beating me; I think it was relief that I hadn't mentioned sexual abuse. Physical and sexual abuse were allowed but talking about it wasn't.

Recovered Memories (memories that I'd repressed)

It's surprisingly common to repress a memory of sexual abuse. Some things are so incomprehensible or frightening that the mind hides it in the unconscious until it can be dealt with safely. Children aren't equipped to handle the trauma of abuse so they cope by "forgetting" about it until a safer time.

One of my recovered memories:

I had a memory of my dad putting his finger inside of me and my legs being spread. I felt the roughness of the shag carpet on my bottom. I was sitting on the platform his bed was on while he sat across from me. He had pornographic magazines spread open on the floor next to him. The bedspread was a houndstooth patterned fabric and my mom had made matching drapes. I looked at them and felt rage that she tried to cover up the horror of the house with pretty decorating. I felt sick to my stomach and had the sense it came from swallowing semen.

Flashbacks

Flashbacks are sudden "flashes" of some part of the trauma. They are usually triggered by something in the present. Flashbacks can be visual, auditory, or tactile. They tend to be intense and seem as though they are happening in the present.

I was at a friend's house and she was showing me some exercises that she does for good posture. We were on our backs on the floor when she grabbed my leg to position me. I screamed and jumped away from her and burst into tears. I had a sudden flash of being positioned for sex.

Another flashback I had:

My husband and I were having sex and I suddenly saw a man standing to the right of me saying in a creepy tone, "I always wanted a little girl."

Dreams

I had a dream over twenty years ago, which I still remember:

I was kidnapped by three people and taken to a remote place in the woods. It reminded me of a compound for some type of cult. There were two houses that looked like old hunting lodges. I was in the main house and it was made of stone. It was filthy and there were roaches running all around. There was a second house to the left of that house.

There were three main people who were leaders, but there were other men and women who were part of it too and none of them would let me leave. I had the sense that I was there to be passed around sexually.

When my memories started to return, I had this dream:

I was part of a community of people living on a cul de sac. There were three men who wanted to date me, but I knew there was something suspicious about them. I thought I was choosing the safe one to go out with. He was the leader of the community. In my dream, he was Colin Firth. For our first date, he asked me to dinner at his house. I knew he was going to ask me to marry him. We sat at a little white metal table for two that reminded me of ones in ice cream shops. Behind the table, there was a walkway that was surrounded on both sides with white lattice and covered in vines. The walkway seemed like something that was used for wedding ceremonies. It led to the bedroom.

In the next scene, I was trying to figure out what was off about this group of people and I organized some of the kids to be spies. I was in the bedroom of the man I was supposed to marry and there was a tall wooden chest with drawers that was built into the wall. I knew there was information in there that had some answers, but before I could open it, the man walked in. The kids had told him I was snooping. Then I became a prisoner.

This dream reminded me of the house and street where I lived when I was 8-10 years old. Most of my recovered memories take place during those years.

I think Colin Firth was in my dream because I had watched *Mama Mia*, where he played one of three dads. I believe that his role represented my dad. I felt so defeated in the dream when I found out the man I picked was the most dangerous one. I thought I couldn't trust myself. There was also the disappointment of trusting the wrong people to help me, who turned out to be on the bad people's side.

There were three main people in both dreams. In the first dream, three who kidnapped me and in the second dream, three who wanted to date me. I know the main leader represents my dad because he was the one in the main house. Previously, I recovered the memory of my next door neighbor, who raped me in his basement with a pool cue. His house was to the left of ours, which corresponds to the second house in the woods.

These dreams seem to represent the sex parties and the other people involved in my abuse.

125

Dreams & Nightmares

Dreams & Nightmares

Dreams & Nightmares

Recalled Memories

The Rescued Soul

Recalled Memories

Recalled Memories

The Rescued Soul

Recovered Memories

Remembering My Past: Memories Journal

Recovered Memories

The Rescued Soul

Recovered Memories

Flashbacks

The Rescued Soul

Flashbacks

Flashbacks

The Rescued Soul

17
Building a Relationship With Myself: Daily Journal

After years of suppressing emotions and thoughts about abuse, I was disconnected from the parts of me that made me—me. Relationships are built through regular communication. Daily journaling has been an excellent way to build a new relationship with myself—a relationship that's founded on honesty and vulnerability. It's an opportunity to check in with myself every day and ask, "What am I feeling?" "What am I thinking about?" "What matters to me?"

Use this journal section however you like. There is one healing insight for every day of the year, but that doesn't mean you need to finish in a year or read one every day. You are free to read them consecutively or you can skip around to find one that you relate to.

Some healing insights are encouraging or inspiring. Others are validating, yet may be painful. Some may bring up fear or anger. You will likely identify with some of them but not with others. It may remind you of something that happened to you or how you thought or felt about your abuse. Or it may trigger another thought entirely.

Sometimes, I don't know what I want to write about. I only know that I feel stirring inside of me that I need to get out. When I don't have the words, I'll write something like, "I feel a tangled ball of bleeehhhh!!! I need to get it out!!!!!!!" Other times, I don't have words but I have a picture in my head that describes it better. I'll write that.

Another way I unblock my feelings is to ask myself when I first started to notice that emotion (or tangled ball of emotions). What happened? Often, that shows me the trigger and I write about that. Sometimes, it's a series of events that all have a common theme like "I feel like all the people closest to me don't have time for me right now. I feel rejected." Then I ask myself what else I feel. Does that trigger a fear? Anger? What's under the anger?

"I have something I want to communicate but I don't know what to say" echoes the feelings I had as a child. I didn't have the vocabulary (even if I'd had permission) to talk about my fear, my pain and my anger. When I stay with the feeling and patiently coax it out, I'm telling the child that I once was that her words are worth hearing.

139

The Rescued Soul

Your healing journey is custom made by you according to what you need. Write whatever you feel. Or don't write. Your healing is in your hands so it's up to you.

Suggestions for using the writing prompts:
Do you agree?
Disagree?
Do you relate?
Does it remind you of something?
How do you feel about it?

Daily Journal

<u>Day 1</u>

To focus on other people's boundaries—their behavior, their responsibilities, their choices, their beliefs, their opinions, their feelings, their attitudes, their values—is to assume responsibility for them. When I was occupied with trying to placate my parents or mend things with them, I was abandoning my own boundaries. I'd already lost so much of myself to the abuse. I needed to accept my parents' right to reject me, which helped me shift my focus onto me.

Day 2

I was criticized for being such a people-pleaser but my well-being depended on making everyone happy when I was a child. My compliance and good behavior were attempts to manipulate my abusers into treating me better. People asked, "Why do you care so much about what people think?" I was conditioned to care. Controlling people's attitudes about me was survival.

Day 3

Over the course of my adult life, I've had a lot of friends who turned out to be abusive, but there was one in particular who was the worst. She drove me to do more even when I was exhausted. She constantly belittled me and kicked me when I was down. She didn't follow through on her commitments to me in favor of doing things for others. That "friend" was me. I was my own worst abuser until I discovered what a wonderful, valuable person I was under all the lies the abuse told me about myself. Now, there's nobody who treats me better than I do.

Day 4

On the days when healing felt particularly difficult, I reminded myself of who I am. I'm that little girl who survived hell and chose to keep fighting through every day. I'm the child who had the will and the strength to go on in spite of being alone. Those qualities are in me. I don't have to strain to put them on or make them up. I'm a fighter. That's who I am. The same strength that helped me survive is helping me thrive.

Day 5

One of my memories felt too disgusting to tell anyone. It haunted me to be alone with the memory, but I couldn't tell anyone either. I started out by just saying I'm keeping something to myself that I'm not ready to talk about. I imagined myself talking about that and got used to it that way. Eventually, I told two people and it wasn't so bad. Then I was able to open up a little more. It's all just a little at a time and being gentle with myself. I didn't have a choice about what happened to me but I do have the choice of how and when I talk about it.

Day 6

When I was a child, I had to sit at the dinner table until I ate all my peas. How did I think I had some sort of say in whether or not I was abused? If I didn't have a choice of saying no to certain foods, I certainly didn't have a choice about my dad putting his penis in my mouth.

Day 7

I used to feel shame when I was mistreated, as though it exposed my worthlessness. Standing up for myself was impossible because of the lies I believed about myself. Then I felt even worse about myself for "letting" people walk all over me. Seeing the truth about my value has given me permission and motivation to stand up for myself. I feel like I'm not only standing up for me, but also for my inner child who never had anyone to defend her.

Day 8

Because of the violations of boundaries of the abuse and because of such dysfunctional family relationships, I really didn't know where I started and stopped. My self flowed into my abusive parents. I identified with their feelings and circumstances more than I did my own. It felt so disloyal to talk about my abuse; I felt the pain of it as though I were betraying myself.

Day 9

I tried to change my thinking patterns for years. I found that the only way to truly "think positive" was to confront the negative thoughts instead of trying to cover them up. Those "negative" thoughts were the parts of me that were never heard and they continued to fight for recognition and expression. Sometimes, they expressed themselves in very harmful ways until I found out what they were trying to tell me.

Day 10

Spiritual abuse interfered with my healing from sexual abuse. When I talked about my painful past, I was told to "Put it in God's hands" instead of feeling and expressing my feelings. I wasn't fulfilling the spiritual standards otherwise. They took away permission to feel and express my emotions, which was a violation of my boundaries in the same way the sexual abuse was.

<u>Day 11</u>

My truth comes out in my story but I am not my story. The things that were perpetrated on me were a reflection of the abuser, not of me. Nobody and no actions have the power to define me. Even though I've defined myself in false ways for many years, that didn't make them true. Healing has allowed me an identity apart from my abuse.

<u>Day 12</u>

My healing starts with validating my wounds and my pain. Part of validation is to stop excusing my abusers through my self-blame. Placing the blame on my abusers doesn't have anything to do with punishing them or seeking revenge. Whatever the consequences of their actions, I'm done with them. I've invested too much of my life on my abusers. My healing is about my life now.

Day 13

Abusers invest so much effort into their self-preservation and their fight for survival. It would be wonderful if all abuse survivors invested as much into themselves. The abuse tells us we're not worth the effort, that we're not capable of improving anything or having any impact on our own lives. We turn against ourselves in shame. Abusers groom us to feel that way because it keeps us compliant and silent. In spite of the lies of abuse, the truth has a way of shining even into the darkest places. Survivors are stronger than the lies and we do find healing and freedom!

<u>Day 14</u>

Since I'm no longer covered in shame, I can see my faults without panicking or turning against myself. I don't feel the desperation to fix my faults or the urge to cover them. I can accept them as part of me—whether a temporary or permanent part of me—and still feel comfortable and lovable.

Day 15

Part of denying my abusive relationships in childhood and adulthood was separating the incidents. I didn't look at the whole relationship, so I didn't notice a pattern of abuse. In my mind, every abusive act was a one-off. I reasoned, "That wasn't nice, but they usually treat me well."

Day 16

When I told my dad that my husband was abusing me, he told me, "But he loves you." When I confronted my dad for sexually abusing me, he told me that he loved me. The "love" I knew gave my abusers freedom to abuse me while I was a prisoner to it. I couldn't get away because they "loved" me.

Daily Journal

Day 17

You may be looking at all the results of the abuse and see how weakened you've become, but some people wouldn't have lived through what you've lived through. And some would have given up somewhere along the way, but that's not who you are. You're a survivor and you'll find a way through this just like you found a way through the abuse.

Day 18

Having a support system in times of crisis is vital. After being alone with your pain for so long, you deserve to recieve comfort from others. It's also important to have people around you who will celebrate your breakthroughs with you since celebrating victories alone can be just as isolating as the pain.

Daily Journal

Day 19

It's generally accepted that you have to stand up to bullies or they won't back down, but when the bully is in your family, you're expected to "let it go." There's especially a social taboo associated with standing up to parents. Part of turning a blind eye to parental abuse comes from denying that parents are capable of causing harm to their children and from excusing abusive acts by claiming it was in the name of love and "for your own good." Overlooking harm done by parents is a way to cope with the pain of their betrayal. Refusing to face the pain leads to being victimized again, which adds more pain. Inside or outside of the family, ignoring bullies doesn't stop them.

Day 20

Being judged for "airing my dirty laundry" doesn't deter me. The truth is more than just the "dirty" experiences of my past. The truth is that there is freedom and healing in spite of the past.

Day 21

I tend to attract people in my life who share the same view of me that I have of myself. When I believed that I wasn't as worthy of respect and love as others, I attracted people who reinforced that belief and I was treated abusively. The more I saw the truth about my value, the more I started to surround myself with people who treated me as an equal.

Day 22

Once I started healing and making changes in my life, I recognized the connection between my childhood abuse and the ways I abused myself in adulthood. I felt so robbed, especially to know that I'd participated in my own destruction. Forgiving myself was the only way I could move forward. I needed myself as an ally to really heal.

Day 23

When I went from using a gas stove to an electric stove, I burned a lot of eggs. I didn't conclude that electric was bad. I concluded that I needed to learn to use it. That's the way it is with anger. Anger is constructive, protective and life-affirming in the hands of those who are skilled. It was up to me to become skilled.

Day 24

I used to neglect my body and resented taking care of it. When I started having health issues, I got mad at my body for letting me down. I felt like it failed me when I was weak or in pain. I'd say things like, "My kidney is giving me trouble again." The truth is I'd given my kidney trouble, not the other way around. I didn't give my body what it needed to thrive and it's done the best it could with what I provided. Acknowledging that helped me repair my relationship with my body so my body could heal.

Day 25

If I had a friend who constantly told me that my pain doesn't matter, I couldn't be close to that person. I can't have emotional intimacy with myself as long as I'm invalidating my own pain. Every time I lie to myself, saying, "That was no big deal," or "You don't have anything to complain about," I'm betraying myself.

<u>Day 26</u>

Instead of admitting that I was a helpless child, I envisioned myself having power. I tried to have a sense of control through self-blame. As long as I did that, I remained a victim to the past. Self-blame kept me a victim. When I finally acknowledged that I didn't have power when I was a child, I could empower myself to make necessary changes in my present life.

Day 27

Leaving my family was painful but the pain of leaving was so much easier than the continual pain of remaining with them. This way, the pain is dissipating instead of perpetuating. I wish I would have seen all the damage those unhealthy family relationships were causing sooner, but I'm thankful to see the truth now. I'm proud of the progress I've made by finally taking a stand for myself. Through my parents, I received the gift of life. Only by leaving them did I develop that gift.

Day 28

When I lost my parents, I was aware that I might have a tendency to fill the void with other people who might not be very healthy. I knew I had to go through the grieving process instead of using other relationships to cover my pain. I made new friends, but I was careful not to put unrealistic expectations on them by putting them in a parenting role or any other role that would give me a "fix". The more I healed and learned to meet my own needs, the more I was able to allow my relationships to develop naturally.

Day 29

On most levels, I accepted that I would likely never have a relationship with my parents, especially my mom. But on another level, it was hard to give up hope that she'd eventually come to her senses. In reality, I could never trust her again. Why would I ever want to settle for a relationship with someone who values me so little? Yet there was this little girl's voice inside me pleading, "Mommy, please love me!" It was a complete fantasy because what I wanted wasn't possible. I still had a hole in my soul that longed to be nurtured. To let go of the fantasy, I shifted from looking to my mother to nurture me to looking to myself.

<u>Day 30</u>

There are children whose hearts are being broken right now and those who are being cherished and adored. I've had to rescue the little girl in me whose heart was broken and give her the cherished treatment she deserved all along. I may not have gotten it earlier, but I can have it now.

Day 31

I no longer look to my abusers with expectation of remorse, or an apology or restitution or restoration or relationship. I'm at peace, accepting that they won't and can't help me out of the mess they created. But I'm the best qualified for that job anyway and I'm happy with the job I'm doing.

Day 32

People started respecting my boundaries when I started believing that I had a right to set those limits—when I truly believed that I was worth protecting and that it was my responsibility to do the protecting. Even when they don't honor the boundaries I set, it's not their responsibility to do so. It's my responsibility to honor my own boundaries by protecting myself from further harm in whatever way is appropriate. In some cases, that might mean moving my desk; in other cases, it might mean leaving the relationship.

<u>Day 33</u>

It's easy for some people to say, "just tell," as though it's best to disclose every-thing. But it's naive to think there aren't consequences. There are valid fears that were meant to protect my life, just as there are fears of the past that limit my life. What helped me to know if I should move forward in sharing a vulnerable part of my abuse is to acknowledge the fear and then ask myself if it's exclusively a fear from childhood or if there are present day consequences. It's amazing how that little exercise has helped me see the truth so I can make decisions I can live with. Sometimes, self-love means telling but sometimes, self-love means keep-ing things private.

Day 34

In my relationship with my parents, they had all the rights while I had all the responsibility. They were entitled to receive and it was my duty to give. They could claim my loyalty; I was expected to prefer and protect them above anyone else—even myself. When I realized how unfair that was and said no to it, it was freeing but it was also painful. When I stopped performing for them, then I had to face what I feared (and had actually experienced) all along, which was their undeniable abandonment.

Day 35

Abusers use any excuse to power over their victims. They justify their punishment by finding a so-called weakness. The weakness doesn't even have to make sense. The flaw could be "too fat" or "too skinny," "too pretty" or "too ugly," "too stupid" or "a know-it-all." I've lived under the control of many abusers and each one considered different qualities a weakness. I learned to fear punishment when others noticed imperfections in me. It's not their right to criticize me or punish me for not living up to what they think is right. I deserve to be treated respectfully, no matter what flaws I have—or I'm thought to have.

Day 36

It was important to my self-image that I acknowledge my past. Before my memories resurfaced, I saw how damaged I was but I didn't see all that I went through and what I survived. Once I really took an honest look at my history, I was stunned that I could not only live through those things, but that I could be a wonderful, caring person in spite of the cruelty of nearly my entire family.

Day 37

For a long time, I wanted my parents to finally see me and the pain that I was in. It felt like I couldn't move on unless they understood and apologized. Unconsciously, I thought if they'd acknowledge me, they'd take away the pain that I felt for being dismissed and pushed aside as a child. But that kept me under their control the same way I had been as a child. They were never going to help me to heal. I found out that they weren't the key to my healing and they weren't even a part of my healing. I was the one who needed to validate my pain and to comfort it. That was when I really started to heal.

Day 38

Unfortunately, when most abusive families are confronted with the truth, they don't choose to heal. Instead, they blame the victim so they can continue in their dysfunctional ways. They don't want to face their own internal demons so they demonize whoever triggers them. Their attacks only confirm how abusive they are and have been. Healthy families can discuss grievances in peace; abusive families don't have the kind of openness or vulnerability that healthy confrontation requires.

Day 39

My silence wasn't good for anyone—even for my abusers. Those types of secrets are destructive to everyone who keeps them. Truth doesn't destroy people or families; lies do. For incest to occur in a family, it takes more than just an abuser and a victim. It's part of an entire dysfunctional system. Exposing my abuse gave the entire family an opportunity to heal and to learn more healthy and functional ways to relate to each other. It was their choice to continue to live in the lies, but that doesn't mean they were "harmed" by the opportunity for another way to live.

Day 40

There are two kinds of pain that come from the truth; there is the pain from dodging it and the pain of facing it. Refusing to deal with it leads to more pain. The more I ran from the truth, the more abuse I encountered—from others and from myself. As I've faced my pain—the pain from things done to me and the pain I've caused others and myself—I've moved through it. On the other side of grieving is joy with life affirming decisions and behaviors.

Day 41

Abuse has such an isolating effect. We're even separated from our true selves. One of the things that helped me feel less alone was hearing the stories of survivors and talking about our shared experiences and emotions. As I connected with other survivors, it helped me to reconnect to myself.

Day 42

Sometimes, in the depth of my pain, words seemed inadequate. I'd wrap my arms around myself and rock or I'd groan or make other sounds when I couldn't articulate something. That validated the pain and comforted me even if it didn't make sense. Later, the words came when I wrote (if I was patient!) But before the words spilled out, the simple act of sitting with myself and grieving silently validated my emotions in a way that nobody else ever did.

Day 43

Surviving the abusive system meant that I learned "my place." I believed that placating abusers was the way to achieve peace. There were rules to follow and as long as I was good, I'd be safe: Keep quiet; don't expect better; don't question anything; don't resist. Conflict was life threatening and there was no standing against it. Abusers always win, which meant more punishment if I didn't cooperate. I adapted by becoming very sensitive to other people's moods so I could fix them before something bad happened. It's no wonder I grew up a people pleaser.

Day 44

I didn't question the rightness or wrongness of the abusive system—I just accepted it. I tried to live in peace by being peaceful, but that didn't work. I was victimized more, not less. There was no pleasing abusers. In all my efforts, in all my experience with a lifetime of abusers, not one ever stopped hurting me because I finally "won them over" by being good enough. Whatever I did, they always found ways to criticize me so they could punish me with more abuse. I wanted peace, but they wanted power.

Day 45

As a child, my only hope of survival was to gain acceptance. Now, I'm a capable adult and I won't die if I encounter conflict. Others' displeasure won't kill me and their rejection won't harm me. I don't have to go along with things I don't like and I don't have to be quiet. When I stopped fearing the consequences of conflict, I learned to oppose abuse.

Day 46

Years ago, I thought the most frightening thing in the world would be to stand up to abusers. But the willingness to stand toe to toe with an abuser isn't where I needed the most courage. I showed the most courage when I started to stand up to the lies within me—when I began to challenge the false messages I learned from the abuse. When I was finally able to confront what really happened to me and really understood the truth, confronting abuse outside of me became much less difficult.

Day 47

I talked about my abuse because I needed to know what happened to me really mattered. The way I was treated as a child told me that my feelings didn't matter—that I didn't matter. I was wasting someone's time since I was a waste of time. The horror and tears on a friend's face told me that what happened to me really was bad and that I wasn't making a big deal out of nothing. What happened to me was wrong. I deserved to be treated better.

Day 48

As I've talked about my past, I've come to accept that it really happened. After repressing the memories of my traumatic childhood, it was unbelievable that the images in my head really happened—and they didn't just happen to someone, they happened to me. I went over it again and again—in my mind and with others. Sometimes, when I shared my story, I felt like a liar even though I knew I wasn't making it up. I'd go in and out of denial and then at some point, I really got it. Talking about my abuse helped me accept the truth. This wasn't a television show or news story—this was my story.

Day 49

I found it so hard to believe my family would hurt and betray me. I'd concocted such a fantasy about who they were that it was a shock to see the truth. My family doesn't hinder me anymore, though they have sure tried. It was easy to get away from them physically but getting away from the dysfunctional thinking and behavior that they taught me has been a process. The more I change my belief system, the less influence they have and they really can't keep me down anymore.

Day 50

The closest thing to love I had as a little girl was from my dad. Even if I had to trade my body for a little attention and affection, my dad was the only source of anything that resembled love. Even though I didn't like what he was doing to me, I felt more security from him than I did from my mom. Telling wasn't an option when I was being abused since the punishment for breaking my silence was that I would be completely abandoned by both of my parents.

<u>Day 51</u>

Every step in the direction of healing, validation, and self-care is a powerful step, no matter how small.

Day 52

"She believed she could, so she did." In the beginning of my healing journey, I didn't have this kind of confidence. I wasn't sure and I didn't know the way but I did have hope and that's where I started. It turns out that hope was all I needed to start. It kept me going until I did build confidence and I could believe. Now, nothing can convince me healing isn't possible or worth every second I've invested into it.

Day 53

When I discovered the multitude of effects from my abuse, the ways I coped, the ways I adapted, I was mad. It was bad enough to suffer the abuse when I was a child but the effects followed me. But the more I thought about it, the more relieved and hopeful I became. Understanding where my feelings and behaviors came from told me that I didn't think and act that way because there is something inherently wrong with me. Knowing that they began somewhere told me that they could also end. I wasn't stuck with them forever.

Day 54

The more I recognize all I lived through, the abuse I faced alone as a little girl, the more I see what a strong person I am. That tells me that I'm more than capable of facing whatever life brings now. I used to compare myself to others and think I was weak, but recognizing the truth about what I was able to live through was liberating. Comparatively, the rest is easy.

Day 55

As I've opened the door to my buried pain and healed it, I've also opened the door to joy and wonder. I have a much deeper response to nature and to children and the things I used to overlook. My life is full of delight in simple pleasures. When I was avoiding the pain, I was actually avoiding my life and many of the most enjoyable parts of it.

Day 56

The abuse taught me that I wasn't acceptable the way I was. To avoid rejections, I made it a habit to study others to figure out what they wanted and conform to their desires. I thought that would make me more likeable, but it had the opposite effect. I eliminated the possibility for real relationships by constructing a barrier. Through my recovery, I removed the shame that hid the real me. I know I'm lovable and acceptable just the way I am and my authentic relationship with myself allows me true relationships with others.

Day 57

When I broke my silence, it was as though a dam burst. After living with secrets and lies so long, it was difficult the keep anything a secret. I started sharing too much information, even to complete strangers. It took some time to realize that total transparency didn't serve me any better than living with the secrets did. Now I know that being true to myself doesn't mean I have to voice every thought or feeling I have and I've learned to share my truth while still protecting my privacy.

Day 58

I used to reconcile with people who repeatedly did hurtful things to me without confronting them. I thought the passage of time was enough. I reasoned that "It happened a long time ago" and assumed that they were sorry and that they'd changed. I also believed that if too much time had passed, I'd lost my opportunity to talk about it. It was as though there was a relationship statute of limitations. But the effects of the abusive treatment didn't expire with time. Neither did my need to be heard.

Day 59

All my life, I jumped from one abusive relationship to the next, each time believing that I'd finally found someone good, someone I could trust. I was too desperate from previous trauma to look carefully where I was going. Every abusive situation left me less trusting of my own ability to care for myself. My need to take responsibility for my own life increased, but my confidence to do so decreased. It seemed easier to turn my life over to someone else rather than face almost certain failure by working out my own way. I craved a hero to rescue me but I had to learn to be my own hero.

Day 60

One day I wasn't feeling well emotionally or physically. I was tired from over-working and from being around draining people. I heard myself say, "I wish someone would take care of me." In the past, I'd had that thought and wondered why nobody did take care of me, but this time, I knew I was that someone. I was asking me to take care of me. Now I know that I don't need permission to nurture myself. I can pamper myself and care for myself the way I wished for others to do.

Day 61

When I have a pain in my body, it means there is an injury or weakness that needs my attention. The pain isn't the problem; the pain is telling me where the problem is. The same is true for my emotional pain. Recurring emotional pain reminds me, "Don't forget to deal with this!" Denying or covering the pain doesn't eliminate it; only attending to my wounds does that.

<u>Day 62</u>

I falsely believed that if my parents didn't love me, I wasn't lovable. I was determined to get their love and approval as though my life depended on it. All of the work I did to try to earn their love was one of the most futile efforts of my life; working through the lies that I believed about myself and learning to love myself has been the most rewarding.

Day 63

The beginning of my healing journey was shaky and unsteady. In every step I took, I got stronger and more confident that I was making progress. The ground I covered in previous steps prepared me for the next steps. Looking back, I noticed that though the issues became more difficult as I progressed, they didn't overwhelm me like they used to. The issues were bigger but facing them became easier.

Day 64

While I was still being sexually abused by my dad, my parents insisted I have a good attitude. I was struggling just to get through each day yet I learned to smile through it. After rejecting my "negative" emotions for so long, it was a major shift to learn to accept my moods and emotions no matter what they are. It's okay not to be happy sometimes. Now that I let out the painful emotions instead of covering them up with a happy face, I'm much happier. The real way I've found to be happy is to let myself be sad. I became a much more positive person when I let myself be negative.

Day 65

The way I used to overwork myself communicated to me, "Others are more important than you are, so keep working even if you're tired, even if you're in pain." I worked and worked to try to escape my badness, but the overwork only validated the lie that I was unworthy. Now that I know that my value isn't related to how much I do or how well I do, I take much better care of myself. I work according to what's best for me instead of how much people need me. My nurturing work schedule is my declaration to myself that I'm just as important as everyone else and I'm my first priority.

Day 66

As I faced more truth in my recovery, I was afraid. I realized that as fearful as I was, my parents were even more afraid. I'm dealing with my issues but they refuse to deal with theirs. They've blamed me for the things they've done and run away from the truth. I used to think I was so helpless and they were so powerful but I'm the brave one and they are the cowards.

Day 67

I used to think that the goal of healing was to eliminate the pain. Pain was an indication that something was wrong, but pain wasn't the real problem. The real damage from my abuse came from the lies I believed about myself: "I'm disgusting," "I'm not worthy of love," "I deserve to be treated like trash." Believing those lies is what caused the pain. Pain was only the symptom, so treating it never solved anything. When I recognized that pain was an indication of a wound, I started using it to help me locate the lies. Once I confronted the lies, accepted the truth and expressed my pain, I didn't need the pain anymore and it left.

Day 68

I was very intentional about the type of environment I created for myself during the beginning (and most vulnerable time) of healing. My recovery has been like being pregnant with my true self so I avoided things that might hurt the new life being formed within me. The two major issues I focused on were my physical surroundings and my relationships. I spent a lot of time resting in a cocoon-like refuge that I prepared in my home and I cut back on social obligations. I also cocooned myself with safe and supportive friends who nurtured me. I refused to spend time with others who didn't feel safe. Giving myself the space that I needed allowed me to focus on the healing work so I could progress through it more easily.

<u>Day 69</u>

Part of healing from my abuse is experiencing the pain I was never allowed to feel or communicate. I was locked up with those feelings for most of my life and the stifled emotions were suffocating me. I thought I was being strong to hold it in but I used all my energy to suppress it so I didn't have much left for anything else. To express pain is to let it out. Expressing it allowed it to leave my life.

Day 70

The abuse taught me that I had no value apart from serving others. I didn't believe that I had permission to care for myself so I cared for others in the hope that they would take care of me. I was always disappointed and felt used and exhausted by my efforts. As I've confronted those lies and realized how valuable I am just because I exist, I'm empowered to make my self-care my priority. Now I know that I have choice about who, when, what and how much I want to do things for others. When I serve others now, it's not from the hope that I'll be cared for in return; it's out of the satisfaction that I've already cared for myself.

Day 71

In the beginning of my healing journey, I was afraid of being re-victimized. Some people thought I was overly sensitive or reactive. It was often difficult for me to distinguish between current abuse and unresolved wounds of the past. I gave myself permission to set temporary boundaries that seemed excessive. My boundaries didn't mean that the other person had done anything wrong, only that I needed a safe place to hear my heart and figure out if I was in a relationship with an abuser or if I was reacting to the pain of my past (or both). The more I affirmed my feelings and made my safety a priority, the more I could trust myself to keep me safe and the less I feared being victimized again.

Day 72

Some people claim that blame is a "wasted and negative emotion." That wasn't true for me. When I placed the blame on the perpetrators of my abuse, I finally had permission to direct the anger toward them, where it should have been directed. Until then, I directed it inward or in indiscriminate places. Expressing my anger in the place it needed to be expressed allowed me to work through it so there could be an end to it. As long as I directed in all the wrong places, there was a never-ending supply of it. By placing blame, I made positive steps toward healing.

Day 73

When I first started healing, whatever recovery breakthroughs I had, however I grew, whatever I faced, it wasn't good enough. I always wanted to be healthier than I was. I thought if I was happy with my progress, I'd become too comfortable and I might quit. I believed I needed to be hard on myself to motivate me to keep going—the same motivation that was used on me by all my abusers. I've learned that being gentle with myself and working at a comfortable pace is not only more loving, it's more effective. I can't heal from abuse while I'm abusing myself through the healing process.

Day 74

I used to beat myself up for not telling when I was a child. I realized that all children tell, even if they don't verbalize the abuse. I had all kinds of ways that signaled that something was wrong, but they were ignored. My mother didn't notice, didn't ask me, didn't want to know. Intuitively, I knew my mother wasn't going to protect me if I told her. My mom's reaction when I disclosed my abuse as an adult verified that. It wasn't my fault for not talking about the abuse while the abuse was going on. It was my parent's fault for not providing a safe environment for me to be able to express that.

Day 75

Before I started healing, I never considered being alone as an option. I was still operating from my childhood fears of abandonment. My experience taught me that being in a relationship meant that I'd have to be abused. I craved relationships so much that danger was just the price to pay. I thought I was bad at picking the right people to have in my life. In truth, it's not that I didn't have any red flags, it's that I couldn't afford to acknowledge them and heed them since I was desperate for connection. I kept telling myself it would be okay, as though I knew it wasn't going to be okay.

Day 76

I've slowly taken my life back from the pain and effects of abuse. Contrary to what it might look like, it wasn't one big decision to heal from my past. It was a lot of little decisions in the right direction that eventually turned into resolve and determination. There are huge rewards in healing, but they are gained by taking little steps.

Day 77

I felt so cheated out of a "normal" life and desperately wanted the abuse and all its effects to go away. It's not fair that someone else violated me and I was left with the effects. I wasn't the one who chose this and I shouldn't have had to address these issues. I decided that despite how unfair it was, I'd already lost so much to the effects of abuse and I damn well wasn't going to lose anymore by not healing.

Day 78

It's frustrating for a spouse to see all the suffering and to experience all the unsettling moments, but that doesn't mean a spouse has the right to short-circuit health and well-being. As survivors of abuse, we didn't ask for this—the abuse, the effects, or the challenges of the healing process—and we don't have anything to apologize for. Spouses sometimes need outside support to face their own issues with this, but they don't have the right ask us to compromise our well-being to relieve their discomfort. To them, its disruptive to their peace; to us, it's life or death.

Day 79

I learned to survive my abusive childhood by studying people and anticipating my abusers' next moves so I could protect myself. As I grew up, I continued to focus on my abusers as a way of coping. I made excuses for my abusers' intentions and found "causes" for their actions so I didn't have to face the pain of abandonment. The trouble was, the effects weren't minimized if they "were doing the best they could." No matter my parent's reasons for the way they treated me, my experience was that they abused me. It was validating to finally be on my side.

Day 80

After a lifetime of shutting down my feelings, it felt overwhelming to face the emotions that came up as I faced my past. I was afraid of being swallowed up by them as though my emotions and the abuse were the same thing. It would have threatened my life to fully feel them as a child and I was still reacting out of the same fear when I ran away from them. I'm an adult now and my emotions don't pose the same danger. Just as skillfully as I buried them as a child, I can unbury them now.

Day 81

When I refer to "when my family rejected me," it wasn't really an event. That was when their actions were so unmistakable that I couldn't make excuses for them anymore. The truth is, their rejection was a lifestyle. They treated me as though I had to earn a place in the family. I hid the truth from myself for a long time by separating their treatment into isolated incidents. As I connected the times they'd rejected me, it became clear to me that I wasn't actually losing them when they walked away from me; I never had loving parents to begin with.

Day 82

Objecting to my family's abuse felt like I was changing the rules in the middle of the game. I'd played by them all my life so it seemed unfair to stop after so long. But the rules I was playing by were their rules. Going along with them so I could survive wasn't the same as agreement. Even if I had agreed to the abuse, it's not unfair to have a change of heart. What is unfair is how they treated me all those years. I had every right to start playing by my own rules—rules that are based on equality, not on my abusers being the only ones who could ever win.

Day 83

My abuse taught me that my thoughts, beliefs, feelings and experiences were invalid. Just feeling something wasn't acceptable; I had to justify how I felt. When it came to setting boundaries, I thought I needed "proof" of some kind of violation or wrongdoing to separate from someone. As I learned to trust my own feelings, I gave myself permission to back off from relationships that didn't feel good. Not feeling good was proof enough.

Day 84

My mom told me that I was living in a fantasy world if I thought my dad abused me. In that moment, I knew what it meant to be invalidated. I felt like she could erase me with her dismissal. I panicked as though she really could snuff out my life by denying what happened to me. As a child, it really was life threatening to me that she ignored the signs of abuse. I needed to acknowledge that my fear was real, but I also needed to acknowledge that my life isn't in her hands anymore. I don't need her to see the truth for me to live. I know the truth and I'm secure in that now.

Day 85

People thought that by telling my story over and over, that I was living in the past. The truth is that the more I talked about it, the more separated I felt from my abuse and my abuser. The secrets kept me imprisoned. I was locked up by my dad's rule not to tell and I shared a bond with him as long as I kept that secret. It was as though I belonged to him. Talking about my abuse was an important part of reclaiming myself so I could move forward. Talking about my past didn't keep me there; it allowed me to move out of it.

Day 86

For most of my life, any hope for my life improving was attached to someone else: I hoped my parents would stop controlling me and trust me to make good decisions in my life; I hoped my husband would share financial decisions with me; I hoped my boss would tell me his expectations instead of criticizing me for not meeting them. My life didn't improve until I stopped waiting and hoping for others to change. It was a revolutionary thought to hope that I could be the one to make the most difference in my life. That's when the improvements came—when I started to hope in me.

Day 87

I felt like the pain of my past would swallow me up so I constantly tried to outrun it. I ran to food or buried myself in work or other activities—anything to keep it from catching up with me. Running from my pain echoed the same abandonment that I experienced in childhood. My parents couldn't tolerate my pain and left me alone with it. As a child, abandonment was a death sentence. It said, "You're not worthy of protection or security; comfort or shelter." To cope with the agony and terror of that, I ran. I ran for my life. Every time I refused to acknowledge my hurt or comfort my pain, I was adding to my abandonment. Healing required me to stop running, but it felt like to face the pain was to die. Learning to sit with my pain and to care for myself like I should have been cared for as a child has been the most validating part of my healing.

Day 88

When I started my recovery, I felt guilty for being a burden to my husband. I wasn't the most stable person to live with as the issues of my past continued to surface. I tried to keep my issues to myself, but they leaked out. Trying to hide my intense process in such an intimate relationship produced a lot of pressure, which only led to more upheaval. Eventually, I told my husband about the pressure I felt and asked for his understanding and patience. He was glad that I communicated how I felt and what I needed. Knowing I had his support, I was able to face my issues more effectively, which benefitted both of us.

Day 89

Some time after my parents rejected me, I reluctantly admitted to myself that I still wanted parents. I judged myself for still wanting their love, as though that made me weak. I confronted my fear that desiring a relationship with them meant that I'd go running back to them and their abuse. I could acknowledge my inner child's desire for a mom and dad, yet I could listen to my adult me saying, "It's not good to be around those people unless they change."

The Rescued Soul

Day 90

When I was married to my abusive husband, I took a certain pride in honoring my lifelong commitment, no matter the cost. I recognize that there was a lot of self punishment in my belief that, "You made your bed, now lie in it." Now I know I deserve a life, not a life sentence.

230

Day 91

The reason I chose healing wasn't because I couldn't cope well with life or that the pain or effects were overwhelming; I chose healing because I wanted to be as healthy as I could possibly be. I suffered enough during my childhood and into adulthood because of the abuse. I wanted something better for my life. I deserved better. I didn't deserve to be burdened with the recovery process, but the effects of my healing have given me the life I'm thrilled to live.

Day 92

I never wanted to be caught feeling sorry for myself or having a pity party. I minimized and dismissed my abuse and my emotions the same way my parents had. It was vital to my healing to acknowledge that I deserved to be treated with kindness, compassion and respect. I needed to validate that I truly did have something to heal from. Now I know it's right for me to have compassion for myself, even if nobody else did—*especially* since nobody else did.

Day 93

When I stood up to my parent's abuse, a few people asked me, "What kind of example are you to your children?" and "If you don't honor your own parents, how do you expect your children to treat you?" Standing up to my parents was one of the best things I've done for my children. Previously, I'd modeled compliance to abusers and unquestioning submission to authority. They'd been raised in a dysfunctional system and learned to adapt to it. Once I objected to abuse, it wasn't long before my daughter did too. I've encouraged my children to protect themselves from any abuse, no matter who it's coming from. If I were abusing them, I'd hope they'd stand up to me the way I did with my parents.

Day 94

My abuser manipulated my body as a way to manipulate my thinking and to shame me into submission. My dad didn't stimulate me for my benefit; it was for his benefit. It made me feel like a participant rather than a victim. He not only violated me, but he turned me against myself. I'm not manipulated by that lie anymore. I'm not to blame for how my body responded.

<u>Day 95</u>

Part of my recovery was to mourn the little child I never got to be and for my lost adulthood stolen by abuse's effects. As I've grieved, I've also made room for new possibilities. I've gotten to know the real me and I'm discovering the joy, the fun, and the wonder of the life I lost.

Day 96

One of the things that hindered my healing for years was the pressure to forgive my abusers. To rush me to forgiveness minimized my abuse, invalidated my feelings and violated my boundaries. I was taught that it was for my benefit, not for my abuser's, but it wasn't for my benefit to be pushed. I needed time to sort through my feelings and then to decide for myself without guilt from outside sources. Every survivor deserves true support instead of being "helped" by conforming to someone else's beliefs about what is healthy for them.

Day 97

I used to have a fear that I'd be obligated to stop talking about my abuser if he was sorry, as though that changed anything about what he had done to me. Now I believe that if there are consequences for his actions, it's not up to me to protect him, no matter what his intentions and actions are now. No matter what happens after the abuse, I still have a right to tell my story—even if my abuser is remorseful; even if my abuser turns into a loving person; even if my abuser builds wells in impoverished countries; even if I restore a relationship with my abuser; even if my abuser is incapacitated; even if my abuser dies—I still have a right to tell my story.

Day 98

It was important to decide for myself how far to go in disclosing my abuse, especially how publicly to share it. Abuse destroyed my boundaries and trained me to put the interests of others before my own. It taught me that I'm less important than others and to serve and give at my expense. By speaking out, I'm bringing awareness to horrors that have been hidden and ignored for too long. I feel good about contributing to something so important, but if it weren't validating for me, I wouldn't do it. I don't owe it to anyone to share my story. It doesn't help stop abuse if I'm abusing myself to talk about it. I only talk about my abuse as much as I feel comfortable. It's my story and I'll tell it in my way, in my timing, and only to whom I choose.

<u>Day 99</u>

The saying, "Whatever doesn't kill us makes us stronger" minimizes abuse. It takes responsibility from abusers and takes credit away from survivors. I was the one who had the will to go on when I was completely alone as a child being abused in my own home. I was the one who endured abuser after abuser as I matured into an adult because of the vulnerable condition from my childhood abuse. I was the one who chose to keep fighting for my life as I've made my way through the process of healing. Whatever resources I had for getting through that, they are a part of me. I didn't get them from the abuse. The abuse left me in a weakened state and it was only because I've worked on my healing for years that I'm functioning now. Good didn't come out of the abuse; good came from overcoming it.

Day 100

When I told my mother that I wanted a healthier relationship with her, she "put me in my place." Even though I stood my ground, I felt guilty and it was a struggle not to be shamed into submission. I felt like I was right back in my role as a child. It somehow felt wrong for her to treat me that way, but only because I was an adult. The fact is, feeling like a child shouldn't feel shameful. Being younger and smaller doesn't mean inferior in value. It was a few years later that I finally recognized that it was wrong for her to shame me when I was a child, too.

Day 101

There are so many complicated feelings to sort through when you're abused. During my earlier stages of healing, I realized that I could have more than one feeling about the same thing. That was astounding to me because all my life, I'd been emotionally repressed so it was a luxury to have even one feeling. Also, I was trained that the only emotions that were acceptable were "positive" ones. I felt out of control when I had conflicting feelings. I realized that fear came from having to pick the "right" one. I felt pressure to feel the way I was "supposed" to feel. I learned to stop judging myself for how I felt and to tolerate the messiness of all my jumbled emotions as I processed them. Now, I celebrate my wide range of emotions, even when I'm experiencing them at the same time. My emotions connect me with myself and with the rest of the world and I appreciate them all. They're a part of what makes me–me!

Day 102

My journey of healing from childhood sexual abuse has really been a quest for truth. I've connected the dots about my childhood, I've made sense of my dysfunctional family, and I've admitted the reality about my mom and dad. But the truth that has made the most difference to my wholeness isn't about the things that happened to me or about other people. My abusers told to me lies to protect themselves and to keep me compliant; the abuse itself gave me false messages; I told myself lies as a way to cope with the confusion and pain. Facing those was painful, but the most precious truth of my healing wasn't painful at all; it's joyful and wonderful. It's the reality about me. Under all the shame and self-hatred was the lovable and valuable person I really am. That was a truth worth discovering.

Day 103

There are people who say that overcoming sexual abuse isn't possible. That saddens me. I know how overwhelming the pain can be; I know how completely invasive the effects of abuse are. Claiming it's possible to overcome doesn't minimize the damage. Abuse left my life a wreck. I hated myself, my relationships were abusive and dysfunctional, I sabotaged anything good and I was afraid all the time. Abuse taught me that I was powerless and incapable of making any type of impact, even in my own life. But abuse LIES! I was capable of healing and so much more. I don't spend my life trying to outrun abuse or its effects anymore. I use my time and energy on really living. Overcoming sexual abuse is hard work. It's the hardest work I've ever done, but it's completely worth it! Survivors of abuse deserve a joy-filled life. I wish I could erase all the pain and damage from abuse from everyone touched by it, but healing is in the hands of every survivor. All I can do is inspire hope. If you don't have any hope for yourself, borrow some of mine. I believe in you!

Day 104

I had control issues all my life, especially as more abuse issues surfaced. When another memory was about to surface, I'd go into a cleaning frenzy in an effort to make everything perfect. It was a way for me to feel control over something in the face of my overwhelming emotions. As I've dealt with the original issues, I've naturally let go of those coping methods. When I notice my controlling behavior, I ask myself what I'm afraid of and get to the root of the fear. Facing the origins of the fear helps me gain my power back instead of using control as an illusion of being empowered.

Day 105

To my abusers, the act of setting appropriate boundaries was viewed as hostile aggression. They believed that I was denying them something that belonged to them if I resisted. I was a resource to be exploited for their personal use. I was property that didn't have any rights over my time, my energy, my body, or my possessions. I viewed myself that way too. I believed that they were justified in being angry with me for saying no but I wasn't justified in being angry with them for abusing me.

Day 106

When I first started my journey of healing from sexual abuse, I got a lot of advice from (mostly) well-meaning people:

"Just let it go"

"Forgive and forget"

"Leave the past in the past"

I didn't find any advice very helpful. It wasn't advice that I needed. I needed people to listen to me and to sit with me in my pain instead of telling me what to do. Living in abusive power and control dynamics throughout my childhood and most of my adulthood, I had very little power over my own life and decisions. I didn't need one more person to decide what I should or shouldn't do. I needed the freedom and encouragement to make decisions for myself.

Day 107

One of the messages from my abuse was, "You belong to me and I can do to you what I want." What I wanted, what I needed, what I felt, what I thought didn't matter. Anyone who wanted a piece of me owned me. I knew myself as property to be used instead of as a unique person to be loved. Abuse demolished my sense of self, which isolated me from myself and from others. How can anyone have a relationship with property? I was lost to myself and to the world until I saw how I came to believe the lie that I was a non-person and recognized the truth that I am valuable, precious and worthy.

Day 108

When parents reject and abandon a survivor of abuse in adulthood, it's an indication of abandonment in childhood. Even for survivors who weren't victims of incest, many were groomed for their sexual victimization from the devaluing treatment from his or her family. They were made vulnerable to abusers by being starved for emotional connection at home or because the abuser knew the child had no protector, no advocate, no ally. Parents don't suddenly become intolerant because of abuse disclosure. If they aren't there for you now, it's not likely they were ever there for you.

Day 109

I used to believe that feeling comfortable around someone meant that person was safe, though "comfortable" people often turned out to be abusers. As I started to heal and to examine that, I saw that familiarity and comfort aren't the same. I was familiar with abuse since I was forced to comply to it. I wasn't relaxed or at ease with abusers; I just learned to tolerate them because I hadn't had a choice.

Day 110

When I used to talk about myself or my abuse, I heard a familiar accusation: "You just want attention." Those words echoed from my childhood. My parents' dismissal told me I was undeserving of attention and I should be ashamed for asking for it. As time passed, anytime I ever got attention, instead of feeling validation, I felt guilt. I was "wasting someone's time" since I was a waste of time. Once I dealt with the origin of that belief and the shame, I could enjoy attention without the accusations.

Day 111

As a child, I was emotionally abandoned if I cried or expressed "negative" feelings. I learned that I wasn't worthy of love and acceptance unless I was happy. As an adult, whenever I felt sorry for myself, I rejected myself the same way my parents had. I hated myself for exposing my "badness" and "making" people walk away from me. I abandoned myself during the times that I needed the most comfort. Healing those wounds allowed me to see that I'm worthy of love even when I express my pain or talk about the awful things that happened to me. No matter anyone else's response to me, I have compassion for myself.

Day 112

I used to enter relationships feeling like "damaged goods" so I settled for being treated that way and usually ended up with even more damage. Now I know that I may need extra space for my healing and I'm still dealing with some effects of the abuse, but I don't need to apologize for what happened to me. I'm just as important as anyone else and I'm just as valuable as I would have been if I'd never been abused.

Day 113

No matter a person's relationship to me, they don't have a right to control me. The intensity of someone's love doesn't give them any special privilege to take my freedom from me. Love doesn't mean, "I know what's best for you and you need to listen to me." No amount of affection or devotion earns them a piece of my life.

Day 114

One of the hardest things for me to accept was that my mom doesn't love me and that I couldn't do anything about that. For a long time, I blamed myself for being so repulsive to her. I thought if I could find my defect and eliminate it, she'd finally embrace me. Then I blamed my dad. I thought if he admitted to sexually abusing me, my mom would suddenly love me. But I was making excuses for her with the hope that something might change. The truth is, if a mother doesn't love her child, it's not a problem with the child; it's a problem with the mother. My mom is free to make her own choices and she didn't choose me.

Day 115

I thought the bonds of marriage and the bonds of blood were too strong to break. I didn't see that the people who told me they loved me weren't really loyal to me; they only used those ties to hurt me. My life started to heal when I chose to be loyal to myself and to honor my bond with me. No marriage vows or family ties are more valuable than my life and well-being.

Day 116

I used to reject and punish myself when I was rejected by others. I thought their treatment was proof that I was worthless. Even though the way I was treated as a child told me that I'm deserving of abuse, healing has shown me that I'm not defined by how people treat me and that I'm just as worthy of equal value as everyone else. Now, when I experience disappointment from the way people treat me, I take special care of myself with comfort and protection. I express my pain in a healthy way.

Daily Journal

Day 117

After all the losses I'd already experienced and the all times I'd had a broken heart, I thought I couldn't afford to find out if my present relationship was real. How much pain and loss could I handle? But the more I thought about it, I'd already experienced so much betrayal and harm that I couldn't afford to settle for another relationship that wasn't based on love. I had to confront my fear that I'd be abandoned if I asked for real love.

Day 118

A person raised in a healthy family is equipped to live a confident and independent life; someone from an unhealthy family is filled with fear and self-doubt. He has difficulty with the prospect of life without someone else. The devaluing messages of control and manipulation create dependency so those who most need to leave their family of origin are the least equipped to do so.

Day 119

When I don't want to do something and it seems unreasonable that I procrastinate or avoid it, it's often my inner child who is objecting to it. When I stop trying to force her to do something she doesn't want to do and listen to why she doesn't want to do it, I can resolve it. Sometimes her objection comes from her fear of the past and she only needs my comfort and assurance. Other times, she objects out of wisdom. She serves as intuition since she doesn't disregard and reason things away the way my adult self does.

Day 120

The decision to set boundaries with my abusive parents didn't have anything to do with whether or not I forgave them. Out of a distorted view of boundaries, some people assumed that I had to be bitter or have hatred toward my parents to cut off my relationship with them. That's not true. It didn't have anything to do with my feelings toward my parents; it had to do with my love for myself.

Day 121

I never used to let myself cry unless I could define my precise emotion and determine why I was feeling it. I had to have a "good" reason. Staying logical gave me a sense of control, but it also kept me separated from my Self. Now I let the tears flow. Crying gives me the release that I need, whether I know the cause for the tears or not. Just sitting with myself and reassuring myself that I'm here gives me the comfort that I need. I didn't get that kind of care as a child, but I'm giving myself that kind of care now.

Day 122

Insensitive people discounted my pain by telling me things like, "Others have it worse." Yes, there are worse things that happen to people. Does that mean the only person who deserves comfort and support is the one person in the world who was hurt the most? Does another person's increased pain diminish mine? Does increased pain make a person more valuable or worthy of care? The abusive system taught me to invalidate my pain but I no longer devalue myself the way others did by comparing my pain or my experience to someone else.

Day 123

The fear of abandonment forced me to comply as a child, but I'm not forced to comply anymore. The key people in my life did reject me for telling the truth about my abuse, but I'm not alone. Even if the consequence for telling the truth is rejection from everyone I know, that's not the same death threat that it was when I was a child. I'm a self-sufficient adult and abandonment no longer means the end of my life.

Day 124

I don't remember ever feeling safe when I was a child. I was continually vulnerable to my dad's sexual advances. I preferred small, enclosed places like blanket forts or my bedroom closet but when my dad wanted me, he found me. Part of my self-care now is being very intentional about creating safe spaces in my life. I've designed cozy spots in my home that are beautiful and nurturing, but one of the most important spaces I've reserved for myself is the space of time. I schedule time just for myself when I'm not available by phone, text, email or any other means. Nobody has unlimited access to me now—not even my husband, not my children, not my best friends. I never had sanctuary as a child, but I'm my own sanctuary now. And I feel safe.

Daily Journal

<u>Day 125</u>

One of the most significant ways I've objected to abuse is when I confronted my dad for sexually abusing me. I knew there wasn't much chance of any change of heart or action on his part, but just speaking up was liberating. I've never felt so empowered in my life. I didn't feel any smaller when he refused to apologize or admit his crime. It wasn't about his response or lack of response. Standing up for myself was an expression of what I already knew about myself—I matter. I knew that no matter what he did or said, it didn't define me or inform me of my value.

Day 126

When I started to talk about my abuse, I was terrified of some horrible punishment. I believed that my parents deserved protection and that some unstoppable force was on their side so they couldn't be opposed. I thought they were completely justified in whatever they did to me since I was without any value or rights. There was no abuse since you can't abuse a Nothing.

Day 127

As a helpless child being sexually abused by my dad, I survived by convincing myself that I could do something to stop it. I couldn't face the truth that I was completely at my father's mercy. I told myself that I was powerful, so powerful that I controlled my dad. I was bad and that's the only reason my dad stuck his penis in my mouth. I wasn't a victim, my dad was. I just needed to figure out how to stop being bad and I could stop the abuse.

Day 128

I used to be the helpful one in most of my relationships, yet I could never ask for help. I was afraid being turned down. The message I heard was, "Who are YOU to expect me to help you?" My fear that people only kept me around for what I could do for them would be confirmed. As long as I believed that I was less valuable than others and that others had the power to assign me value, I was stuck, but now I know my value. Nobody else determines my worth and I'm important apart from anything I have to offer. I can ask for help now. If the answer is no, I don't take it as a blow to my worth.

Day 129

Loving touch is necessary for human development and continued health in children and adults. Part of the abuse was harmful touch but it was also the damage of not being touched in loving ways. It wasn't only the abuse that needs to be healed. I never enjoyed being touched other than in sexual ways. Part of my healing has been to reconnect to my body and begin to enjoy pleasurable non-sexual touch.

Day 130

The abuse told me that my needs weren't important and that I was on the planet to serve someone else's needs and desires. I used to feel so heroic for putting everyone first, but that was just a coping method. It was a way to romanticize and validate my dysfunction. Now, I know I'm important and I take care of myself first.

Day 131

One of the benefits of my healing process is that now I show up for my life. I'm fully present and engaged inside and outside of me. The key to being present in this moment is that I examined the things in my past that kept me stuck there.

Day 132

Setting boundaries in relationships felt dangerous. I tolerated poor treatment since that was better than finding out that they didn't really love me. I was willing to settle for their version of love since that was better than being alone.

Day 133

Even if I can't connect my feelings to a particular source, I acknowledge my feelings and validate them and express them. After a lifetime of suppressing, ignoring, discounting, criticizing and hating my emotions (and myself), it's healing to listen to and to comfort myself the way I craved for others to do for me all my life.

Day 134

Bringing shame on the family doesn't come from disclosing abuse; the shame comes from the shameful acts perpetrated on its members. "Airing dirty laundry" isn't the thing to be afraid of. The things to fear are the dirty secrets continuing from one generation to the next.

Day 135

Even when I learned that the coping methods that saved me when I was a child were hindering me in my present life, they weren't things I could just shed overnight. The child within me panicked over losing the things that helped her stay alive. To stop coping, I had to replace those unhealthy habits with the love, comfort and nurturing that I lacked.

Day 136

I thought my silence was "for the good of the family." Now I see what a sick system I was protecting. What's so sacred about a group of people who destroy the most vulnerable among them? It's not something that should be preserved.

Day 137

When my parents walked away from me, I felt incredible pain. But what exactly did I give up? Those people weren't "family" to me the way family is supposed to be. I'd clung to an illusion. It took a lot of grieving to realize how much better off I was without the people who required me to earn the so-called love they dished out.

Day 138

I've found so many ways that my abuse defined sex incorrectly, which led to me abusing myself in other relationships. I thought sex would produce allies since in my childhood, being compliant equaled being safer. So whenever I felt threatened, I offered sex.

Daily Journal

<u>Day 139</u>

My dad telling me that he loved me used to work very well to keep me compliant. "Love" meant I wasn't allowed to object. I believed that love equaled ownership and as long as someone loved me, he could do whatever he wanted, while I should just be grateful to be loved. That fed into my belief that abuse was all there was to a relationship. Love meant being hurt.

Day 140

Embracing my anger is validating. It's a declaration that I deserve to be treated better. When I feel anger, it's a reminder that I'm valuable and worthy of protection.

Day 141

When my dad stopped sexually abusing me, I felt loss. Suddenly, my dad wasn't giving me much attention anymore. I felt the same pain as a relationship break-up. When I finally admitted that to myself, I felt guilty. I thought that meant I wanted the sexual abuse. As I worked through it, I realized that since my dad was my only source of love and affection, it was a real loss. I wanted the love, not the abuse.

Day 142

By confronting the way I learned to think of myself through my parents' eyes, I began to love myself and have compassion for myself. Now, I don't wait for them to change their opinion of me since I don't need them to see the truth. I see the truth about myself now and that set me free.

Day 143

When the truth is hidden, abuse flourishes. When the truth is revealed and accepted, it has the amazing ability to set people free. The lie is that pain can be avoided in the midst of abuse. But there will be pain. The question is: Will it be the continuing pain of the lies or the diminishing pain of healing?

<u>Day 144</u>

There are people who say, "It happened, it's over and done with and there is no use in continually hashing it over because nothing will change the past." It's true that it's not possible to change the past. That's not the purpose of validating my past. Validating my past is part of healing, which has the ability to change my future.

Day 145

Many people who saw my cycle of abusive relationships believed that I deserved whatever I had coming to me for "allowing" it. But I'm not responsible for my abusers' actions. That thinking comes from misunderstanding boundaries and taking responsibilities that were never mine to take. It's unhealthy to accept the blame for anyone else's feelings or actions. It's healthy to place the blame back on the perpetrator.

Day 146

You can't have a healthy relationship with an abuser. Abusers must dominate. Everyone is either a superior or a subordinate; there are no equals. Abusers have no sense of personal power so they gain power by controlling others. Their personal worth is achieved by one-upmanship. If you try to assert your own power with an abuser, he will escalate until he wins.

Daily Journal

<u>Day 147</u>

The game you play with an abuser is really war. He may make light of things, "I was only joking," or "You're being too sensitive," but each move you make to explain yourself or question him is seen as an act of hostile aggression. The abuser thinks in terms of defending his territory. Attempts you make to understand the situation is a challenge to his power. He rarely shares his thoughts, feelings or plans and you don't get the clarification you ask for because in the abuser's eyes, that would make him vulnerable.

Day 148

As I heal, I see more of myself—the real me. I'm no longer fooled into seeing the things that I do as me. I can relax and do nothing without feeling that my existence is threatened.

Day 149

As a child being abused in my own home, I didn't have the option of avoiding the abuse even if I knew it was coming. To survive, I stopped listening to myself. As an adult, I still ignored my internal warning. That "something's not right" feeling meant nothing to me. After all, I still believed that I was powerless to do anything about it.

Day 150

As an adult, whenever I talked about the past, I hated myself for exposing my "badness" and "making" people walk away from me. I expected to be abandoned the same way my parents had abandoned me and I abandoned myself during the times that I needed the most comfort. Seeing where those beliefs and behaviors came from allowed me to see that I'm a worthy of love even when I express my pain or talk about the awful things that happened to me.

Day 151

I learned that I wasn't tolerable unless I was happy so I learned to shut up about my needs and my pain. Acting like everything was okay was the only way to avoid more pain from rejection.

Day 152

I feared pain as though the pain was worse than the thing causing the pain. Pain is meant to remove us from harm; it's supposed to alert us so we can move in the opposite direction. But as long as I was suppressing my pain instead of removing myself from the source of pain, I stayed in danger even though I finally had the power to protect myself.

<u>Day 153</u>

When I was a child, I didn't have power over very many things. I didn't decide when people would hurt me and I couldn't make it stop. I couldn't make my mom pay attention to me. But I did find solace in a few things like food. So escaping the pain through food gave me some sense of comfort and control. Back then, that was my only choice. There was no way to improve my life in any real way so numbing the pain was the only option. My goal in life became to go in the opposite direction of the pain since I couldn't succeed at anything else.

<u>Day 154</u>

The more I reparent my inner child, the less I've felt like an orphan and the less I feared abandonment. I was abandoned, but I'm not anymore. Being less dependent allows me to choose better boundaries and healthier relationships.

Day 155

I was committed to finishing my process and I knew that experiencing the pain was instrumental in that. I needed the pain to tell me where the wounds were so I could nurture those areas and they could heal.

Day 156

Anytime something bad happened to me, I felt shame. From haircuts gone wrong to being laid off at work to being rear ended in my car, I believed it was all the consequences for my badness. Every negative experience was confirmation that I was undeserving of love, pleasure, safety, respect, or comfort.

<u>Day 157</u>

The thing I've noticed about most healing advice is that it's dissociative. It encourages the survivor to separate from their own feelings and/or to disconnect from the truth. It's also a disconnection of the advice giver from the recipient. Instead of connecting with the survivor's pain in an empathic way, advice is dispensed from a safe distance. It's a substitute for real, human connection. It keeps things rational and intellectual instead of getting into the messy emotional stuff.

Day 158

To avoid abandonment, I'd accepted the responsibility for my entire relationship with my parents. If there was something that needed to be repaired, I needed to do it. After they left, for the first time in my life, I had to accept that I was powerless to convince them to love me or to treat me better. I needed to accept my parents' right to think for themselves and decide their own priorities. I needed to respect their right to discontinue their relationship with me. I needed to accept their no.

Day 159

I had a "normal" relationship with my dad for years even after I remembered that he had sexually abused me. Why wouldn't it be normal? He'd abused me for years while I pretended that everything was fine. That was normal.

Day 160

When I first started talking about my abuse, it felt like I was lying. I didn't feel connected to what I knew. It all felt distant and surreal, like a dream. Added to that, I didn't have any emotions about it for a long time. It was as though it happened to someone else. It didn't seem possible to experience such horrible things and not feel anything about it, so on some level, it felt like I was making it up. Eventually, the emotions came and I knew those things didn't just happen, they happened to me.

Day 161

Rescuing myself from the isolation meant untangling the messy net of lies. Lie by lie, I freed myself. Despite all the ways I'd disconnected from myself, I'm a whole person now. I'm delighted with me. I'm good, fulfilling company for myself. I'm a solid presence in my own life. I can connect with others now since I'm connected to myself. I have deeply fulfilling relationships based on truth—who I really am—a unique and lovable person.

Day 162

I thought wearing masks would make me more likeable, but I eliminated the possibility for deep relationships by constructing a barrier. Looking back, I can see why I experienced so much rejection. People couldn't relate to my false front. Even if someone did connect with that false persona, it wasn't the type of connection I longed for since it was based on a lie. I could never have real intimacy. I rejected my true self before I even gave people the chance to accept or reject me. The rejection of my true self led to putting on a false self, which led to rejection by others, which led to more rejection from me.

Day 163

Throughout my life, I reacted to my shameful identity by trying to prove it wasn't true. I "knew" it was true, but I was desperate to escape from it. I wore masks to hide from the awful person I thought I was. I played roles out of some hope of being accepted. I studied people to figure out what they wanted. I conformed. My whole life felt like a performance.

<u>Day 164</u>

I wasn't aware that it was the abuse that told me lies about myself. I thought I was abused because those things were true. I thought I was inherently worthless so I deserved whatever anyone did to me. I wasn't old enough or secure enough in my own self-identity so I was defenseless against the lies.

Day 165

My father's abuse penetrated more than just my body. My very being was contaminated by the false identity it forced on me. My dad's actions were an accusation. Through the abuse, he communicated to me that I didn't have the value of other children. I wasn't worthy of protection. I wasn't worthy of real love. I wasn't a real person; I was an object, only useful for disgusting things and then discarded. I was trash.

Day 166

The separateness that protected me from harmful touch also isolated me from *any* touch. I couldn't sense connection with anyone. I was driven to be with others—not being with someone else made me feel like I didn't exist—but whatever the relationship, I always felt alone. It was as though I lived in a bubble.

Day 167

Though I separated myself from my body in my mind to survive the abuse, it was *only* in my mind. I really can't separate my body from the rest of me. My body and I are one. As I've connected to my mind and emotions more deeply, I've connected more and more to my body. What affects one, affects the other. I'm a whole person, intact, together. I'm with me.

Day 168

Throughout my life, I've escaped from the unpleasantness that was happening with my body—dental visits, medical exams, sex. In fact, even if I didn't "leave" my body, I never really considered myself a resident of my body. I didn't identify with it as mine. It wasn't something I felt responsible for or cared for. I criticized my body mercilessly. When I looked in the mirror, I'd look away in shame for having to be encased in something so fat and ugly.

Day 169

During the early days of my healing, the process was completely exhausting. I couldn't afford anything in my life that was competing with my healing. Eliminating friends who didn't contribute to my growth was just as important as cultivating supportive friends.

Day 170

I took inventory of all my relationship—friends, acquaintances, co-workers, family—anyone I had contact with on a regular basis. I evaluated my feelings about each relationship (not each person—for a lot of them, I really enjoyed the person but the relationship didn't make me feel good). I asked myself three questions: How do I feel about myself when I'm with this person? Do I feel more or less energy with this person? Am I more optimistic or pessimistic about my healing journey with this person?

<u>Day 171</u>

Knowing I'm empowered to improve my life has freed me of my belief that I need to be taken care of by others. Feeling secure in my ability to care for myself, I'm not vulnerable to people who would exploit me. I know I'm free to grow and develop to change my direction. I don't feel imposed upon by other's decisions; I speak my mind and express my needs. I'm no longer driven by circumstances; I'm an active participant in shaping my life.

Day 172

I was afraid of owning my power for fear of becoming an abuser. In fact, abusers operate out of victim mentality, which is the belief that they don't have any power so they take other people's power. Being empowered isn't about powering over someone else; it's about being secure in your own power.

Daily Journal

Day 173

I was conditioned to believe I didn't have any choices. I was a victim in childhood but I'm not a victim anymore. Now, I think in terms of what options I do have rather than what options I don't have. Victim mentality kept me from making empowered decisions but now I own my power to improve my life.

Day 174

I've realized a little at a time over many years that I really am capable of improving my own life in big and small ways. As a childhood victim, one of my only powers was complaining. As I've transitioned into viewing myself as an empowered adult, I've learned to listen to my thoughts. I've become alert to grumbling or whiny expressions that are meant to gain me sympathy—as though I'm completely at someone else's mercy. As I challenge those beliefs, I remind myself of the options I have. Instead of complaining, I act.

Day 175

Working with my inner child has been a key part of my healing. It's not enough to heal the damage of abuse; I also have to provide the nurturing care that I was denied. Reparenting myself does that. I pay attention to the child within me. I listen to what is important to her and give her a voice. I address her fears by protecting her and comforting her. I provide the gentle treatment she never experienced.

Day 176

I used to fit in time for myself between everything else (if at all) and now I fit in everything else after I've taken care of me. I used to hope that someone else would take care of me—that all my hard work would be recognized and someone would designate "my turn". I realized that *is* my turn.

Daily Journal

<u>Day 177</u>

Even when I did pleasant things for myself, it was a chore to complete. The things that most people enjoyed were a burden to me—I was a burden. Just as my mother never found joy in caring for me, I never did either. It really made me sad that I didn't find pleasure in doing nice things for myself. I grieved for how my mother treated me and how I'd learned to treat myself.

Day 178

The best way to express anger depends on the purpose of the anger. What is the anger saying? What was happening when I became angry? What do I believe about the situation? What am I afraid of? Being taken advantage of? Being violated? Being humiliated? Devalued? There is always an underlying feeling and message that I need to pay attention to. In some cases, it's enough to validate my feelings and to release them. But other times, the situation calls for more action. I ask myself how I can use my anger to improve the situation. What is my anger trying to teach me? Sometimes, I need to decide to take better care of myself. I might need to ask for my needs to be met. I might need to confront someone. I might need to adjust my boundaries or my schedule.

Day 179

Sometimes current situations trigger a much stronger reaction than what the situation really calls for. Usually, it's unprocessed anger from the past that is multiplying its intensity. Even if my anger isn't "justified" by the current situation, I don't judge myself for having a feeling. I look at my feelings as clues to what's going on inside of me and use it for my benefit. I ask myself questions. When have I felt this way before? What does this situation remind me of? When I find myself overreacting to my current circumstance, it's an opportunity to heal from the past.

Day 180

The lessons of my childhood taught me that anger leads to pain. Anger meant rejection; it was abusive and out of control. It was emotionally and physically violent. But that isn't the truth. Anger is only a feeling and it can be directed in ways that are constructive rather than destructive. Merely having an emotion isn't abusive. Anger is response that we should have about innocent children being abused or about other injustices. It's meant to motivate us to action. It's a signal to protect others or ourselves from harm. The purpose of anger isn't to annihilate life; it's a tool to preserve life.

Day 181

As long as I rejected and denied my anger, I didn't control it; it controlled me. It spilled out unintentionally on me and others I cared about. Displaced anger is impossible to get rid of. As long as I projected it in all the wrong places, I could never work through it; there was a never-ending supply. Giving myself permission to "feel what I feel" has proven the shortest way out of that emotion. Processing my anger allowed me to resolve it.

Day 182

As I started to take an honest look at my past, feelings that had been buried since childhood began to stir up even more. Anger seemed to bubble out of me. Even minor boundary violations triggered a much stronger reaction than what seemed appropriate. I had trouble being in public for fear of seriously hurting someone. I was reacting to all the times that my boundaries were violated in the past when I was either not allowed to object to (in childhood) or when I believed that I wasn't allowed to object to (in adulthood).

Day 183

After I remembered that my dad had sexually abused me, our relationship continued as it had. I called it forgiveness, but I hadn't even validated my own pain yet. It wasn't really forgiveness since I hadn't faced that there was anything to forgive. I was in denial; I just swept it all away and pretended it never happened. Getting mad about it was very healthy and necessary for my healing. It was a sign that I was finally considering and connecting with me.

Day 184

I buried my anger, but it was buried alive. It scratched and clawed and cried out, mostly through abusive acts toward myself. I also occasionally blew up at people close to me. I didn't relate it to my abuse; I considered it another of my personality flaws that I was born with.

Day 185

Sometimes, the memory of abuse doesn't bring up much emotion, but feelings emerge when I consider the messages behind the actions. I sit with my emotions and express them in whatever way I need to. I cry, write, call a friend, or cuddle up in a blanket. I acknowledge that my feelings are valid and important.

Day 186

There is so much loss to grieve from the effects of abuse. The lies caused me to behave in ways that stole the life I could have lived. I missed opportunities, I sabotaged myself, I stayed in abusive relationships, I didn't raise my children the way I wish I had. I express the anger and sadness over the ways I adapted to the abuse. Grief opens the door to new possibilities.

<u>Day 187</u>

Sometimes, the memories seem to surface spontaneously. Other times, a current event in my life triggers a memory that still contains painful lies that I believe and live by. I've learned to pay attention to either feelings or behaviors that seem to be overreactions. Those are indicators of unresolved issues from the past. When I identify a possible trigger, I ask myself what that event reminded me of. When did I feel misunderstood like that? Or betrayed in a similar way? Or rejected? Immediately, the answer comes to mind.

Day 188

One of the key ways I was damaged from abuse was through the lies I came to believe about myself—mostly about my value. In every memory of my abuse, there are overt messages and covert messages. The overt messages come from things my dad or other abusers verbally communicated to me or about me. The covert messages come from what I deduced from the way I was being treated, rather than from actual words.

Day 189

Abuse is harmful in two ways: It damages us from the bad things that we weren't made to endure plus it denies us the vital things we needed to thrive. Healing deals with both of those things. It repairs the damage and provides the love and nurturing that were absent.

Day 190

Some people claim that digging up events that happened so long ago just keeps us trapped there. On the contrary, looking at my past was the way to rescue myself from it. I was held captive by the beliefs and feelings of my abuse, but going back to examine them freed me.

Day 191

I recognize that the only way to stop being haunted from the ghosts of the past is to confront them. When something triggers me—a smell, a person, a situation, a touch, a place, a word—part of me is a Ghost-Buster, hunting down the things that threaten my peace. But when I walk down the dark corridor of a long-forgotten memory, another part of me wants to run away. Before I'm even conscious of being triggered, the child within me fights as though it's a life and death struggle and screams, "You're going to die! Get away now!" To her, the trauma is ongoing and the threat is current. In that moment, it's not merely a memory, it's happening now.

Day 192

Talking to understanding and compassionate people was the gateway to feeling compassion for myself and acknowledging the depth of my loss. When I finally sat still with my experience and listened to my heart, I finally felt heard. The horror and tears on a friend's face told me that what happened to me really was bad and that I wasn't making a big deal out of nothing. I deserved to be treated better.

Day 193

What I didn't know when I disclosed my abuse is that it's very common for families to reject rather than support the survivor. That's especially true with incest survivors. In incest families, the family system is a culture that protects itself by keeping the secret. That system's survival depends on the secret, so they often sacrifice one member for the sake of the family.

Day 194

Before I compiled my story, I felt disjointed as a person. My past was in little scraps, disconnected and without context. Telling my story was the beginning of understanding myself. The fragments of my past fit together, which helped me feel more "put together" than I ever had. I went from feeling dismembered to remembered. Instead of being stuck in my abuse, clearly seeing my past helped me to finally begin to move away from it.

Day 195

Before I started healing, I was living out of my parents' version of my story. According to their version, I was spoiled and strong-willed and would lie and do whatever I needed just to get attention. I came from a very good family who loved me and did everything they could for me, yet somehow, I turned out bad. That's the story that I believed about myself until my healing process prompted me to question the "reality" that I "knew". Telling my own story was a powerful way to take back my life.

Day 196

Incest gave me an overwhelming sense of isolation. When nobody else was around, *he* could get me. I wasn't only physically alone—unprotected—I was completely without an ally. There was nowhere to run, nobody to hear my cries for help, nobody to believe me or comfort me. In the whole wide world of people, I was deserted.

Day 197

Comfort was the best I could do when I was a child, but I'm not a child anymore. Now that I'm pursuing my well-being over comfort, I have emotional health *and* comfort.

<u>Day 198</u>

My inner child reacts out of her pain and fear and struggle. As an adult, I'm much better equipped to decide the best action to take. I need to rescue her from her abuse-filled world, but before she's willing to come with me, I have to be willing to go to her. I have to sit with her and identify with her experience and emotions. I have to respect her viewpoint and offer her understanding and compassion. That's the only way she'll trust me enough to let me rescue her.

Day 199

Using my coping methods for my benefit requires me to ask, "Am I doing what's best for me now?" I need to decide that from the perspective of an empowered adult instead of a panicked child. That means knowing when to push forward to face the pain and when to back off until another time.

Day 200

Learning what self-love is, I've become more gentle with myself by providing more breaks from the healing process. I've found that my biggest breakthroughs come after I take a break. Numbing myself gives me a repreive from the intensity of healing or other life issues so I can rest. While coping as a *lifestyle* communicated to me, "I can't deal with you! You're too needy!" using healthy coping methods in a nurturing way can communicate, "I notice how tired you are. Come rest for a little while."

Day 201

As a child, it was intolerable to be left alone with my pain. No one held me or told me that pain was normal and not something to fear. Pain meant my mom would push me away. Abandonment was a death sentence. It said, "You're not worthy of protection, security, comfort or shelter." Masking the pain was survival. It was the very best I could do. As an adult, I still believed that pain—and the abandonment that followed—led to death.

Day 202

It really doesn't matter if my parents intentionally hurt me or not; the bottom line is that their neglect and abuse damaged me. Whatever my parents' histories, whatever their motives, they still hurt me and I still have the effects to deal with. As long as I looked for reasons and answers in my abusers, I remained damaged. In the process of searching for the solution with them, I missed finding the solution within me. I had to recognize that no matter how the wounds occurred, they did occur but healing is in my hands. I've made peace with the past, but it's only come through facing the truth—and the truth can't be found in them, but I did find it in me.

<u>Day 203</u>

Instead of admitting that my parents didn't love me, I tried to find some other explanation for the way they treated me. Attempting to understand my abusers was my way of separating from some of the pain. It was a lie to "protect" myself from really seeing the awful betrayal that I suffered. Their present treatment showed me more clearly just how little they care about my feelings.

Day 204

I used to feel sorry for my parents' hard childhood and excuse the way they treated me. It's true that my dad never threw me through a window like his dad did to him, but the things he did to me were equally destructive. Even to say "equally destructive" isn't really relevant. I'll never know everything my parents lived through as children and maybe they did have it worse than I did, but so what? It doesn't matter who was hurt more. Comparisons don't heal anybody.

Day 205

I've heard it said that people are products of their pasts. I understand that the way my parents where treated by their own families handicapped them. But to say they are "products" of their pasts as though they are inanimate objects who don't have any choices about what their pasts "make" of them is an excuse. Yes, they were influenced. There are sick things they were taught to view as normal and things that they weren't equipped to give me because of their own neglect, but they are responsible for their actions, no matter their past.

Day 206

During my abuse, I sometimes "left my body" so I wasn't mentally or emotionally present. I had repeated that during sexual encounters ever since then. When I started working on my sexual healing, I became conscious of connecting on an emotional level with my husband before we had sex. I kept my eyes open and thought about how much he loved me. Before that, intimacy and sex were things that didn't mix for me.

Day 207

When I started having flashbacks during sex, it felt like another violation. I needed to find a way to feel safer. My husband was very understanding and coorperative of my needs. I needed to be more communicative about what I was feeling during sex. If I wanted to take an extended break from sex, I did that. If I wanted to have sex only when I initiated it, that was okay too. The thing that helped my husband was to know that I was truly working on healing and that the work would pay off with a healthy sexual relationship. Meanwhile, we created intimacy in other ways, so our relationship became stronger than ever.

Day 208

I struggled with my sexuality. I had to work out my issues apart from a sexual relationship with either men or women. I wanted sex with men for validation since I thought that was my only value and I wanted sex with women to get the nurturing I craved. Ultimately, I had to find the validation and nurturing inside of me because no relationship could ever fulfill such a huge canyon of unmet needs. Since I was using sex as a means to resolve my childhood hurts, I engaged in sexual relationships from the maturity level of a child. I wasn't ready for that type of relationship since children aren't ready for sex. I was only contributing to more pain. Once I resolved those issues, things became much more clear.

Day 209

I've had a lifelong conflict over sex. At times, I've wished it didn't exist and other times, I thought life wouldn't be worth living without it. I've seen it as my source of power and my biggest weakness. My source of validation and my source of shame. It meant comfort and pain. Resolving my conflict meant I had to sort through each false definition and how my identity and value were mistaken through sex. Now, I can enjoy sex but it doesn't have power over me. Sex is just sex.

Day 210

When a child of an acquaintance disclosed her abuse, I reacted by suddenly being repulsed by sex. I'd loved sex all my life, so that was a dramatic shift. Over the next few days, I told my body that it never had to have sex again if it didn't want it. To my surprise, I sensed a huge relief. I'd never known how much I needed to know I didn't have to have sex. The abuse gave me the message that I didn't have a choice and even though I enjoyed sex, I really needed to be firm in the truth that I didn't have to do it. It took some time to work through it, but giving myself permission just to *be* was incredibly freeing and self validating.

Day 211

I knew that to be loved, I had to have a good attitude. I learned to have a positive attitude about everything—things that I should have run from. I accepted circumstances without questioning them. Instead of making improvements to my life, I improved the way I perceived my life. My optimism helped me to cope with the powerlessness I felt, but it prevented me from seeing things realistically.

Day 212

When I talk about my childhood sexual abuse, I see it as an opportunity to validate my inner child. As I reveal the horror of what happened to her, I'm inviting her out of the shadows of fear and shame. She's accustomed to others' dismissive denial, but telling the truth gives her the honor she deserves.

Day 213

When my parents walked away from me, I partially believed that I deserved it—that I had brought it on myself. It was justified punishment for asking for better treatment. I was just discovering my voice, my value, my rights. Looking back, I hardly asked for anything but I thought it was too much. I was too much trouble. I was too much to bother with. I learned not to ask much of life and just learned to go along with whatever I got.

Day 214

Since I wasn't healthy in the way I was helping myself, I couldn't be healthy in helping others. I had to stop seeking value from what I did and find out the truth of my value just for existing. I discovered that I was worth helping and serving and then I could give myself the focus that I deserved instead of waiting for others to deem me important enough to help. It's a whole different way of living and it's so much better. Now, I'm so much more effective in reaching out to others.

Day 215

For years, I didn't have a clue about my own needs. I didn't know if I was hungry, thirsty, sleepy, sad or if I had to go to the bathroom. All of it got jumbled up and I only knew I felt uncomfortable. My childhood sexual abuse from my father and the emotional neglect from my mother trained me to meet the needs of others, but not mine. My needs were so lost that I didn't even know what they were.

Day 216

Sometimes, I don't have the luxury of putting my commitments on hold while I deal with my emotions. Some parts of my life require more focus and energy than I can afford when I'm engulfed in pain. In the adult world, there are times when it actually is necessary for survival not to be so emotionally connected— like at work. Sometimes, coping methods help me function. In that case, I'm loving myself by protecting my job or other responsibilities.

Daily Journal

<u>Day 217</u>

Part of telling is choosing who you tell and don't tell. You don't have any control over how people will react, but you do have control over who you share it with. You don't have to publish a book or post it online. Talking about your abuse to someone is important, but you don't have to tell everyone and you aren't a failure or a coward if you choose not to.

<u>Day 218</u>

Healing is a long process, but it gets better with every step. After a breakthrough in healing, it's normal to feel a variety of emotions from relief to victorious to depressed to exhausted. I'm careful to be gentle with myself every time I take another step in my healing. It's part of undoing the damage that was done through the abuse. Abuse sends the message, "You aren't valuable," but good self-care says, "You are precious".

Day 219

I discovered that before I could have a satisfying relationship with others, I had to have a satisfying relationship with myself. I couldn't have that as long as I was covered in shame and self-loathing. I needed to see the real me instead of the lies my abuse taught me. I needed to sort through those lies and accept the truth so I could see my value and love myself.

Day 220

I was clumsy when I was learning to assert my boundaries. I still wasn't sure of my rights, so out of a fear that I wouldn't be taken seriously, I came on strong and had a harsher "no". Once I was confident in my rights and took myself seriously, I became better at saying no much more graciously.

Day 221

I used substitutes for my real needs. I needed rest or relationship or recreation, but I gave myself food or sex or shopping. Since I wasn't supplying what I really needed, I was never satisfied. I needed to know that I deserved to have my needs met and then I had to start asking myself what I really needed and provide those things.

Day 222

When I was still in a relationship with my parents, I didn't question whether or not I needed a relationship with them. Then I figured out that having a relationship meant an abusive relationship. I asked myself, "What was I looking for in a relationship with them?" "Were they the unmet needs of childhood or the adult needs for community?" Whatever I was looking for, I wasn't getting it from my parents anyway, whether I was in a relationship with them or not. I needed to find another way to meet my needs.

Day 223

"Stay the course" became my mantra when I felt like I couldn't breathe through another moment of the struggle. As suffocating as it was, I knew I'd feel even worse if I gave up so I stayed. Many times, all I could do was curl up in my big, comfy chair. That was as strong as I could be—not giving up.

Day 224

After a six year estrangement from my parents, I didn't follow the advice of well-meaning people to "let bygones be bygones" before it was too late. Rushing to my dad's deathbed in the hope of finally getting the love I used to crave would be useless. "Too late" means it's out of my control now that my abuser is dead. But it was already out of my control before he died. The lie is that there was something I could have done to make my dad love me. I tried all my life to earn that from him—to convince him I'm worthy of being loved. It was never in my control. Not in the end, not in the beginning, not in the middle. Never.

Day 225

When my dad died, some people didn't understand why I was grieving. Why would I mourn someone who had caused me so much pain? Through him, I lost my innocence, my childhood, my sense of safety, belief in my own personal power, trust, and much, much more. Through him, I lost my connection to a dad, to my mom, my brother, and for years I lost connection with myself. One person commented to me, "At least you don't have much to miss." But that's not true. There were good times mixed with the abuse and a whole lifetime of loss of the loving father I never had. I found myself missing what might have been. There were so many "what might have beens."

Day 226

Though my dad genuinely seemed to enjoy spending time with me, all of my memories with him are tainted. I'll never know what was motivated by real love and what was grooming me to accept his abuse. The good came with the bad. I learned that love comes at a price and abuse was the price of love.

<u>Day 227</u>

Being so public about my abuse has been costly but I count it a bargain compared with the expense of silence.

Day 228

My hope for relief from abuse seemed to be in pretending I didn't notice. I desperately wanted to be someone who could say, "Is that all you got? You hit like a girl." I couldn't have conceived of chasing off my attacker or in defending myself. The only thing I could imagine was coping better by developing tougher skin.

Day 229

Nobody had to tell me to overlook the ways my parents hurt me. Of course I had to "let it go." It was survival to discount myself. As an adult, those lessons of abuse were so engrained that I was still convinced that I didn't have any other options. When I didn't overlook insulting or degrading treatment, I was punished. Even weak objections were met with accusations and attacks.

Day 230

In a healthy relationship, vulnerability is wonderful. It leads to increased intimacy and closer bonds. When a healthy person realizes that he or she hurt you, they feel remorse and they make amends. It's safe to be honest. In an abusive system, vulnerability is dangerous. It's considered a weakness, which acts as an invitation for more mistreatment. Abusive people feel a surge of power when they discover a weakness. They exploit it, using it to gain more power. Crying or complaining confirms that they've poked you in the right spot.

Day 231

I've been physically, sexually, spiritually, financially, and emotionally abused and the most pain I've experienced is from the emotional abuse. The message of my dad's sexual abuse communicated to me that I wasn't good for anything except sex, but my mother's emotional abandonment—treating me like I was invisible—told me that I wasn't good for anything. With her, I had absolutely no impact. I couldn't do anything, good or bad, to gain her attention or win her affection. It was like I didn't exist. I don't know any pain worse than that. I coped with the pain of having no impact by trying to tell my abusers that *they* had no impact. If I ignored their hurtful behavior, maybe they'd wonder if they had any affect on me, which gave me a false sense of power instead of having any real power.

Day 232

I convinced myself I was the "bigger person" for letting it go. The truth is, I didn't overlook cruelty or rudeness out of a sense of personal empowerment, but out of my belief that I was small and insignificant. My experience taught me to avoid feeling even less significant by keeping my mouth shut. Actually, I wasn't letting anything go. It was all being compacted deep inside of me. While I was telling myself it was all rolling right off my back, it was infecting me, making me feel smaller and smaller.

Day 233

In the midst of sorting out the pain of my parents' rejection, I heard myself think, "Parents aren't important." That stopped me. That's not true—parents are very important, and not just in childhood. I'd lied to myself as a shield from the pain, but I was ready to face another layer of that. My life would have been better if I'd had loving parents, but the way they are, my life is better off without them. I want parents, but I don't need them now. For a few days, I grieved the loss that the new truth brought. It was both painful and empowering. It felt good that I was cleansing myself of another lie and I was proud of myself for acknowledging the truth.

Day 234

When I confronted my dad about abusing me, I felt so empowered to be both gentle and strong. I was firm in speaking the truth and didn't feel bad if the truth happened to hurt him. I also didn't lose sight of my needs even in the midst of my dad repeatedly discounting and ignoring them. Every time I told my dad what I wanted, he changed the subject, but I kept going back to what I wanted. Afterwards, I felt so free that I could tell him how I felt and what I wanted, yet not feel like that made me vulnerable. In the end, my dad's actions told me that my needs still aren't important to him and I was okay with that. My needs are important to me and they are no less valid just because he refused them.

Day 235

In the abusive system, the abuser is the victim and the victim is the abuser. When the abuser does something destructive, it's really the victim's fault for not doing things right. It's the victim's responsibility to keep the peace and to keep the abuser happy so that nobody gets hurt. The abuser has no responsibility.

Day 236

The only thing that stops abuse is standing up to abusers. To stop *being* a victim, I had to admit that I *had been* a victim. I had to recognize how powerless I was as a child under the hand of my father—that there wasn't anything I could have done to stop him. I had to see that it was a lie that I could control an abuser by my good behavior.

Daily Journal

<u>Day 237</u>

Anger is never for no reason. Much of my anger has been rooted in unmet needs or in invalidation. Acknowledging and taking care of my needs helps me deal with my anger in a caring, responsible way instead of turning it against myself or others.

Day 238

I was trained to take care of my parents' feelings in the hope that if they were fulfilled, they'd finally take care of me. I waited for the "validation" for most of my life that my needs were important too, but it never came from them. Their manipulations stopped working when I realized my value and stopped needing their permission to put myself first.

Daily Journal

<u>Day 239</u>

Talking about my abuse allows me to hear myself. As I listen, I hear myself emphasize details that I'd thought were insignificant. It's given me greater understanding of my feelings and behaviors today. I've made connections between past events and current feelings and behaviors. I've solved today's problems by looking back at how I got here.

Day 240

I used to look for validation from other people, but it's the ways I validate myself that really count. It's not when someone else decides that I'm worthy or valuable that I know that I really matter; I know I matter when I do loving things for me.

Day 241

Believing I lacked any ability to impact my environment, the only "safe space" was the false safety I created within my head. I dismissed potential danger; I ignored possible threats. My mantra was "It will be okay."

<u>Day 242</u>

I thought sexual abuse happened the same way hurtful words sometimes slip from my mouth. I never mean to cause any harm but when I do, I feel awful about it and take responsibility. But sexual abuse is never a "slip". Through my new lens of truth, I saw that sexual abusers plan and scheme, seducing their victims to submit and to keep their secret. Not only do they blame their victims, but through their words and actions, they convince their victims to accept the blame. Child molesters are particularly interested in self-preservation and willingly sacrifice the child's physical and emotional health to protect themselves. They are not "nice" people who simply do bad things.

Day 243

My abusers promised me approval and acceptance if I could just do this one more thing. If I did that thing, I would be loved; if I didn't, I wasn't worthy. So I'd sweat blood to do that one thing and then suddenly, it wasn't that thing, it was something else. I was a continual failure in my abuser's eyes and in my own.

Day 244

I was convinced I was a failure, though I was driven to prove I wasn't. I thought if I could do something so great and so big that nobody—not even my toughest critics—could dispute or ignore it, *then* I would really be somebody. In my mind, since my abusers denied me the approval I craved, they were the sources of it. I didn't see any other way to be worthy.

Day 245

The abusive system that I grew up with and continued in for many years taught me that weakness meant death because only strong people are valuable and worthy of life. Only people who earn their way are deserving of love and approval. So I despised my weakness and my entire existence seemed dedicated to covering it up.

The Rescued Soul

Day 246

Where am I in this journey and how much longer is it? It used to torture me that I didn't know where I was in my healing journey—that there was no map telling me, "You are here." I don't think that's relevant to me anymore. Healing is a lifetime commitment the same way all growth is so I'll keep healing as long as I'm alive. I'm healthy and whole even if I'm still working on issues. I am excited to get up most mornings, I'm optimistic about my future, I'm surrounded by healthy people, and I'm good at taking care of myself. I love myself and I love my life. Whatever issues come up in the future, I'll be ready for them.

Day 247

I felt robbed and cheated from the abuses I suffered and out of a feeling of being owed, I angrily asked my husband to prove his love to me. When I felt particular pain or anger from my wounds, I asked him to buy me something or do something for me. My husband is wonderful, but it's not possible for him to make up for what I missed in my childhood. Only I could give myself the love I never got.

Day 248

The introduction to horrors so young impressed on me just how helpless and vulnerable I was. Parents are supposed to empower their children to live without them but in my family, I wasn't given permission to be my own person. I thought I needed them to live and then they abandoned me. It's no wonder I felt so unempowered well into my adult years.

Day 249

I believed I was too sensitive and weak. To "prove" I wasn't a victim anymore, I moved closer to painful experiences rather than away from them. Remaining in harm's way and exposing myself to more pain kept me in the victim role rather than moving me out of it.

Day 250

The childhood sexual abuse taught me that my value came from sex. In adulthood, I was driven to have sex since I always felt worthless. I felt important and desired until it was over and then I felt like garbage—the same way I did after the abuse. I didn't recognize that the bad feelings afterwards were indications that I wasn't treating myself very well. I desperately needed to feel valued again, which led to more sex. My sex addiction only stopped when I believed that I'm valuable apart from anything I do.

<u>Day 251</u>

It doesn't reduce the effects to tell yourself your abuse wasn't that bad. That invalidates yourself and your pain—which makes things worse, not better. Healing starts by acknowledging that what happened to you was awful. You deserve to heal.

Day 252

Nightmares, memories and flashbacks felt like invaders in my life, but the true enemies are the lies and secrets those things are meant to show me. Fighting them not only prolonged them, but ignored their benefits. They can be frightening, but when I welcome them as allies, they provide me with vital intelligence for healing.

Day 253

For years I believed that I was somehow powerful enough to be the cause of my abuse, yet I was too powerless to stop it. Now I see I'm not the problem, but I am the solution. I'm not to blame for my abuse, but I do have the answers to healing inside of me.

Day 254

"Getting over it" comes by surrendering to the healing process—letting the memories come up, expressing the emotions, facing the lies and nurturing myself. I tried to get over it by putting on a happy face and avoiding the memories. It's hard work to avoid the memories and it's hard work to heal, but avoidance makes things worse and facing them makes them better.

Day 255

As an adult, I'm able to be more discerning than my child-self was and better equipped to reject the lies that my abuse and my abuser told me. Yet my adult-self will experience the overwhelming child-self feelings until I confront the lies. I'm not worthless; I'm not dirty; It wasn't my fault.

Day 256

There was nothing I did to "bring it on myself." As an adult, I look back at the futility trying to protect myself from my childhood abuse by behaving or performing a certain way. I never had any control. Recognizing that truth helped free me from the performance-oriented behavior I still lived with.

Daily Journal

Day 257

There didn't seem to be any separation between me and the shame. It wasn't like a tumor that could be removed; it seemed as though the shame and my being were melted down into liquid that hardened into my present self. That's how it felt, but that wasn't the truth. Once I saw how the shame worked itself in—that it was applied to me—I knew it could be removed.

Day 258

I was particularly susceptible to denial until I acknowledged the uncomfortable truths that I'd been hiding from. I didn't see how much abuse I was tolerating toward my children and me. As long as I denied the truth hidden inside of me, I was blinded to the things happening outside of me.

<u>Day 259</u>

Under all the lies about myself that the abuse convinced me to believe, was the real me. As long as I was running from the truth, I was running from me.

Day 260

Triggers can be a useful healing tool, revealing long-buried emotions and in-dicating areas in need of attention. One way to respond to triggers is to pay attention to the specific things that cause a reaction and to give yourself time to express your pain and to console yourself.

Day 261

One of the main lies of abuse is that you don't deserve to be treated well, which makes self-care very challenging to many survivors. Healing is exhausting so it's vital to allow yourself to recharge physically and emotionally. Make a point to do one nice thing for yourself a day. Nurturing yourself is a declaration through your actions that you are valuable and deserving of love.

Day 262

It's common for those who are sexually abused to be abused more than once and by additional abusers. What made us vulnerable in the first place is compounded, so we become repeat targets. Survivors sometimes refer to that as having a sign on them that says, "come get me." For years, I thought that "having a target on my back" meant I was to blame for repeated abuse. It was my fault for "being a victim". While we can repair those broken places in us that make us more vulnerable, being vulnerable doesn't make us responsible or blame-worthy for any abuse. The perpetrator is 100% responsible for his or her behavior. Noticing a vulnerability in someone doesn't equal the right to do harm.

Day 263

As I've become healthier, I've examined the people closest to me. Do they hinder or help my growth? Do they try to pull me back into old patterns or do they applaud my progress and change the unhealthy ways they've related to me? In some cases, I've had to choose between being loyal to a friendship and being loyal to myself.

Day 264

When I was a child, I couldn't decide when people hurt me and I couldn't make them stop. It was impossible to improve my life in any meaningful way so numbing the pain became my mission. That served me then, but as long as escaping pain was my aim, I was distracted from making the kinds of changes that the pain was signaling me to make.

Day 265

Setting boundaries isn't something I hand off to others, as though it's their responsibility to honor them. The truth is, it's my own responsibility to honor my boundaries. I can't control whether or not people will respect my "no", but I can decide what to do if they don't. I can respect my own "no" by taking appropriate steps when my boundaries are violated.

Day 266

Saying yes when you really mean no isn't a good way to cultivate a healthy relationship. Doing so can't build intimacy because you're not revealing your true self. It's a risk to reveal your true feelings, but it's the only way to know if you're loved for you or what you can do for the other person. Saying no isn't a rejection of the other person; it's an acceptance of you.

Day 267

In survivor mode, I adapted to whatever circumstances I was handed as though I had no options. I became an expert at "making the best of a bad situation" and "going with the flow." Thriving after abuse means skillfully managing my choices, acknowledging my personal power, and becoming a proactive participant in my own life.

Day 268

Shame caused a split between me and my body. When I gained weight, I was ashamed to be seen with it. I blamed it for letting me down when I haven't felt well. I felt disgusted when people touched me, not only because I felt threatened, but because I feared contaminating them with my "badness". As I've confronted the lies I believed about myself, I've learned to think of my body as me instead of an enemy that I needed to stay away from.

Day 269

"Just move on" or "The past is the past"? It's naive to think your past doesn't influence your present. The things you learned yesterday affect your thoughts, decisions and actions today. Until you face the past and examine what false messages you learned, you carry those harmful beliefs into the future. Examining the past isn't living there; you live in the past when you refuse to examine it.

Day 270

It's important for me to recognize the way abusers operate, but knowing that has only helped me once I dealt with the beliefs and feelings that continued to make me vulnerable—things like "I'm not good enough" or "I'm not worth protecting." It's not enough to use determination and will-power to save me; I had to make some real internal changes.

Day 271

No matter our beliefs about forgiveness or any other issue, part of healing from abuse is to discover our own way. We were abused by being overpowered and controlled and part of our healing is to break away from that. To be pressured or manipulated to do something "good" for us is not really good for us.

Day 272

As a child, I believed I was bad and I deserved the abuse. I tried to perfect my way to protection. Even as an adult, I tried to perform perfectly, as though my life depended on it. Putting all my energy and focus on perfection diverted attention from actually dealing with the origin of my issues and pain. The lie kept me busy working on something that would never solve anything.

<u>Day 273</u>

I got so tired of people saying "just choose to..." or "just stop..." in regard to the effects from abuse. To say, "just..." anything is to reduce it to a simple choice or a quick fix. Yes, I had to be determined to heal, but healing isn't a matter of willpower.

Day 274

Family abandonment is at the heart of incest and childhood sexual abuse. Sexual abuse doesn't lead to family abandonment; family abandonment leads to sexual abuse. Emotionally dysfunctional parents produce children who feel (and are) isolated. Those vulnerable children become easy targets for sexual predators—either inside or outside the family. Desperate for love and connection, the children are seduced. Without anywhere to go with their pain and confusion, they are driven deeper into isolation.

Day 275

When I notice that I seem to be sabotaging my success, I ask myself "what if" questions. What if I succeed? What if I fail? What if I continue? What do I expect to happen next? What am I afraid of? I used to see my self-sabotage as an impenetrable roadblock, but now it's just indication of a fear to overcome. By identifying my fear and confronting it, I can continue moving forward.

Day 276

I don't believe that "everything happens for a reason." I don't believe that I have to accept everything that happens to me as fate. The awful things that happened to me or the unwelcome events that happen now aren't unavoidable, destined events. To believe that is to remain a victim. As a child, I was under the control and will of greater powers than me. As an adult, there are things that *are* out of my control but I'm not locked into a particular outcome or path; I'm making my own.

Day 277

Supposedly, my parents corrected and controlled me into my adulthood for my benefit. They were critical out of concern that I would sabotage my life if I didn't make the improvements they told me I needed. It's strange how much better my life got after I didn't have the "benefit" of their superior wisdom anymore.

Day 278

I used to blindly follow people. It didn't have to do with trust, though that's what I called it. Actually, I feared that asking questions would be viewed as a threat or an accusation of wrong motives or incompetence. It was the opposite of trust. I feared the outcome of following without knowing more, but I believed it would be much worse if I made myself known as a "troublemaker" by "doubting" or "defying".

Day 279

As a victim, I used to fear abandonment more than abuse so I settled for reconciliation under any terms. Looking back, abusers seemed exclusively concerned about *their* pain over losing the relationship rather than in *my* pain being in it. I don't think that anyone who demands forgiveness or trust deserves either one.

Day 280

"You know how she is" is not an acceptable reason for overlooking abusive behavior. Does that mean that there is some kind of free pass for people who have been abusers for years? Does that mean if you don't object to abuse the first time, you're obligated to accept it forever? As far as I can tell from my own life, knowing that a person is "how she is" doesn't make the abuse any less painful.

Day 281

Expressing my boundaries doesn't mean I'm expecting someone else to change. It means I'm changing. I'm shifting from accepting a certain behavior to rejecting it. Boundaries aren't about controling other people; they are about controling other people's access to me.

Day 282

I noticed that when people suggested that I was too hard on my parents and that I try to reach out to them again, I'd get angry. I knew that kind of suggestion felt very dismissive of my pain and minimized the abuse. However, I also realized that my anger came from feeling the pain of abandonment and wanting a relationship with my parents. I didn't set out to be an outsider in my own family. I don't like being rejected. I wouldn't choose to be ostracized, but as painful as it is, it's still much less painful than continuing a relationship with them.

Day 283

Before I started healing, I felt hollow. I'd covered myself in roles that weren't me and masks that weren't me, but I didn't know who "me" was. How could I become "me" if I didn't even know if there was a "me"? As I discovered, I didn't need to see or "make" myself into anything. I was so used to contorting myself into certain roles that I thought I would "achieve" the real me the same way. In reality, all I needed to do was remove the lies that had been heaped onto me. The truth set me free. I was there all along!

Day 284

Part of healing was recovering my voice. I'd been silenced by the belief that my opinions, ideas and feelings didn't matter and by the fear that I wouldn't express myself intelligently even if I did dare to speak up. Working through the origins of those lies allowed me to see I'm worth listening to. The greatest impact in seeing that truth is that now, I listen to myself.

Day 285

Survivors of abuse intuitively know that the past holds the answers for moving forward, which is why we think and talk about it until it's resolved. I started to move in the direction of healing without even knowing that's what I was doing. I started thinking about it and talking about it and feeling it, but then I was bombarded with all kinds of messages that told me I wasn't doing it right. "I needed to forgive, I needed to stop thinking about the past, I needed to accept responsibility for my part…" Just like my body knows what to do to heal itself from wounds, so does my soul. The challenge was listening to *it* instead of the invalidating advice.

Day 286

I used to feel heroic for sticking with abusive relationships. I believed that "love conquers all", which to me meant that love gave me power. I thought I could make everything better through love. That worked well for my abusers; the worse they treated me, the better I treated them. "Killing with kindness" is really victim mentality. My so-called love was really manipulation. Placating abusers never worked for me as a long-term solution. It perpetuated abusive patterns by validating them. That wasn't love for myself or for my abusers.

Day 287

When I stood up to my mother's manipulative tactics, she demanded that I honor her. Before that, I don't think I even considered how either of us defined "honor". It seemed to mean that my parents were entitled to my subservience. I owed them a debt of honor because of their care-giving in raising me. Today, I have a better picture of honor. I honor my husband out of appreciation for who he is and what he's done in my life, but not out of a position of inequality or subservience. I can honor my husband yet live by my convictions instead of his. My husband has earned a place of honor in my heart, but my parents haven't. I don't owe them anything, especially not honor. I reserve my honor for people who act honorably.

<u>Day 288</u>

I tried positive affirmations for years, but it was like spraying air freshener in a room full of trash. The positive things felt like lies until I took out the trash of my negative beliefs.

Day 289

I used to feel threatened wherever I made mistakes. They felt like a spotlight focused on me. I imagined an announcer booming, "Attention, please! Everyone look at Christina. She is careless and stupid and bad. Take note of her badness and avoid her. Remember that she's a failure so you don't get tricked into thinking she's anything but bad." Now mistakes don't bother me much anymore. I hear an internal voice saying, "Attention, Christina! You are not perfect and you don't have to be. You are flawed *and* loved."

Day 290

After feeling like a nothing, it's taken me years to build a healthy self-identity. I'm secure and complete in myself, unafraid of being alone. I'm sure of my own value apart from my performance, possessions or appearance I know my own mind; I'm confident of my own wisdom; I trust my own judgment. I'm working out my own path, defining my own purpose, and assigning meaning to my own life. My life actually feels like *my* life now.

Day 291

When people used to tell me things like, "leave the past in the past," it was their way of creating distance from me and my pain. I recognize that it was a coping method for them just like running from my own pain had been for me. I understand that when people say things like that, it's out of their own issues and they most likely intend to be helpful, but it was still important to validate to myself the pain it created in me. I'd turned to them for comfort or support, but it triggered the same pain of abandonment that I'd felt from the original abuse. Even if they refused to sit with me in my pain, I needed to sit with me.

Day 292

Before I started to heal, I thought I could detect abusers by how I felt about him or her. That wasn't helpful at all. I felt varying degrees of affection for all my abusers. It turned out that being likable wasn't their only quality. While I was still working on my belief system about what I deserved, I found that a good starting point for me in spotting abusers was asking how I felt about myself when I was with them. Though nobody is responsible for my feelings, it was useful to see what kind of influence they had. If I usually felt bad around someone, I examined them closer to look at the reasons for that.

Daily Journal

<u>Day 293</u>

It's a process to separate from unhealthy relationships. Recognition comes in stages. Even when you start to see the difference between what love really is and what you've been settling for, sometimes it's hard to accept that you're worthy of real love.

Day 294

As a child, it was intolerable to be left alone with my pain. No one held me or told me that pain was normal and not something to fear. Pain meant my mom would push me away. Abandonment was a death sentence. It said, "You're not worthy of protection, security, comfort or shelter." Masking the pain was survival. It was the very best I could do. As an adult, I still believed that pain—and the abandonment that followed—led to death. I needed to provide what was lacking in my childhood—I had to validate my hurt and comfort my pain. When I felt insecure, I needed assurance; when I felt sad, I needed comfort; when I was mad, I needed understanding. I thought I deserved to escape my pain, but I really deserved love.

Day 295

When I was still married to my abusive husband, I had an aquaintance who was married to someone who treasured her. I was so envious that I felt like I hated her. I saw myself as an outsider of everything good. I thought good things were what happened to good people so they were out of my reach. Now, my life is filled with goodness. I started to have hope when I found out I wasn't a bad person after all and that it wasn't a matter of "deserving" good things. I found out I was actually empowered to bring good things into my life instead of waiting for them to happen to me.

Day 296

I used to be so desperate for love and acceptance that I didn't ask myself how I felt about someone who seemed to want me. I thought it was such an honor to have attention from someone. Now, I don't discount my feelings out of the "honor" of being "chosen". If someone gives me attention, I don't owe them anything. I'm valuable because I exist, not because of their acceptance.

Day 297

Examining my inner voice with curiosity rather than judgment allows me to see what is behind my critical thoughts. Through curiosity, I'm a companion to my exploration; through judgment, I'm my own adversary. Telling my inner voice to shut up doesn't help me; it silences my voice, but not the lies. When I follow the trail of the critical voice (What do I believe about that? Where did that come from?), I can get to the validating truth.

Day 298

When I consider how much I love my children, I'm very content knowing that I have such a strong connection with them—relationally and emotionally. I didn't always believe that I was capable of a bond like that. Thinking about how much I miss my children when I haven't seen them reminds me of how easily my mother let me go. What I have with my kids is what I always wanted with my mother. By being the mother to myself that I deserved, I've been able to be the mother to my children that they deserve.

Daily Journal

<u>Day 299</u>

When I was a child, I was treated as though I was selfish for having needs. As an adult, it took a long time to figure out what my needs actually were. I've asked for opinions when I really wanted validation. I've asked for advice when I really wanted to be heard. I've given myself caffeine when I really needed a good meal or a nap. Today, I'm attentive to my needs because I enjoy giving to someone I love.

Day 300

Feeling overwhelmed comes from feeling like things are bigger than me—that I'm not enough. When I'm overwhelmed, I ask myself what feels so much bigger and more powerful than me. Usually, it's several things rolled together. As I face each one separately, it's much less intimidating. The fear doesn't blind me to the resources available inside and outside of me. I see the truth of how empowered I am.

Day 301

The message from abusers is that it's not safe to tell; that's the same message that survivors are given by others when we try to talk about our abuse: "Talking about it will make you feel worse." Or "Why drag all of that up? It will just drag you down with it." Talking about abuse didn't make me feel worse; it helped me get better. Do you know what made me feel worse? Being told not to talk about it.

Day 302

When I tried to envision a future for myself, it was dark and hidden. I struggled to make choices that would shape my life. My abuse taught me that my life was determined and defined by whoever wanted me. It was a lie that they had a right to take my life. Taking back my life has been a long process, but now I know what it means to "be my own person" and my future is in my hands.

Day 303

Having the responsibility to carry the secret of my incest family was much too heavy a burden for a child. Even into adulthood, I struggled to manage the rest of my responsibilities under the secret's weight. By telling the secret, it was as though I handed back the burden to my parents—and the shame that went with it.

Day 304

As the secret-bearer of my family, I was the sacrificial lamb. The rest of my family could go on with their lives and as a family unit as long as I was silent. Breaking the silence meant I became the black sheep. In spite of how painful that has been, I'd still rather be a black sheep than a sacrificial lamb.

Day 305

I used to say that my childhood was not ideal, but not bad. Admitting to myself that it was bad meant that I was damaged from it. But denying the abuse and denying the damage didn't save me from experiencing the effects. I continued to suffer under the damage done through my abuse until I faced it—and the beginning of facing it was admitting to myself how bad it was.

Day 306

In my head, I realize that we live in a world that is full of chaotic events and that good people are killed or treated unjustly every day. I don't believe that when someone is a victim of a tragedy, it means they did something to deserve it. But a child believes everything is personal. To gain some sense of order, when something bad happens to a child, it's because he or she did something to cause it. Even into adulthood, I was still operating from that child-like belief. When something bad happened to me, I believed it was because I was bad.

Daily Journal

Day 307

One of the biggest struggles of my healing process has been self-care. It has been a whole new way of thinking to consider that I am responsible for taking care of me. It's not that I still believed that others should take care of me—it's that I didn't think of it as anyone's responsibility. When the neglect caught up with me, I felt like a failure. That added another layer of resistance to self-care since I didn't think a failure deserved to be treated well.

Day 308

It never feels like a good time to face the pain of abuse. It's a survival method to avoid pain, but I wanted a life that was much more than survival. To thrive, I had to face the pain, but first, I had to have hope of something better. My hope began from seeing the effects of healing in other people's lives and when I started to see it in my own life there was no stopping me.

Daily Journal

Day 309

Children need love to survive and if the real thing isn't available, we find the closest thing. Since abusers often tell us what they are doing is love and some of what they offer feels nice, we accept it as love. If we don't know the real thing, how do we know the difference? Believing that abuse is love is a matter of survival.

Day 310

When someone asked me what I wanted, I used to tense up in fear. What I really wanted was to avoid being rejected so I tried to guess the "right" answer according to what the other person wanted. Considering what I really wanted wasn't relevant because none of my preferences mattered enough to risk rejection.

Day 311

One of the most frustrating questions I ever asked myself used to be, "What do I want?" How was I supposed to know that after so many years of discounting my desires out of a belief that they didn't matter and were out of reach? At first, I didn't know what I wanted, but I did know some things that I didn't want. I started by saying no to those things. I felt like a two year old. That's actually one of the stages where I was stuck so it felt good to establish myself as a separate person by saying no. Eliminating the things that I didn't want helped me to find my own identity apart from others so I could find the things I wanted to say yes to.

Day 312

The message of my parents was, "We don't approve of who you are. You should change to fit in with the family and avoid embarrassing us or yourself." Those views reflect their own shame and sense of worthlessness. It didn't have anything to do with me. Just because I don't fit in with an abusive system doesn't make me unworthy.

Day 313

I used to be drawn to situations that mimicked the chaos I felt inside of me. As I put the external situations into order, it made me feel a bit more in control of my internal chaos. As I became aware of that attraction, instead of using it as a distraction from and a replacement for addressing the feelings inside of me, I used it to understand myself. Dealing with my internal world resolved a lot of the issues in my external world.

Day 314

Others tend to treat me the way I treat myself. In the past, I came to the conclusion that I was to blame for people mistreating me since that's the way I treated myself. I don't blame myself for other's behavior anymore. I know that other people are responsible for their actions and I am responsible for mine. Now I see this bit of wisdom as a reminder to take responsibility for how I think about myself so I treat myself better. Part of treating myself better is to remove myself from the company of people who don't.

<u>Day 315</u>

I thought I could rise above my abuse by pushing it down, but allowing it to surface was the only way I could overcome it.

Day 316

What I called, "pity parties" were really an expression of being stuck in the contradictions of my belief system and emotions. I didn't believe that I had the right to validate my pain or my experience but I felt the pain of it. I believed that I deserved to be mistreated but I felt angry about it. I didn't believe that I had the right or the ability to change my circumstances or to stop the abuse but I felt desperate for relief. My self-pity was a result of my frustration over not having permission to feel compassion for myself. Pity never helped me out of my situation but having compassion for myself did.

Day 317

When someone suggested that I forgive my dad for abusing me, I felt as though that person was minimizing what my dad did. It was as though my dad deserved my forgiveness since the abuse happened so long ago. I felt like the bad one for "carrying a grudge." I felt misunderstood and judged for "being petty." Insisting that I forgive meant my abuser wasn't the problem, I was.

<u>Day 318</u>

Trying to understand the reason why my parents abused me gave me a sense of control. I thought comprehending it would be like fitting it into a neat and tidy little box. Maybe I had misunderstood. Maybe I got it wrong. Maybe they didn't mean to hurt me. Believing that was denial. It protected me from the pain of betrayal. Accepting that my parents had a choice in whether or not to hurt me, that they could have stopped themselves, that they knew they were hurting me increased the pain, but it was the truth. Denial doesn't lead to healing; facing the truth does.

Day 319

A lot of people seem to associate victim mentality with "making a big deal of nothing," but it's actually victim mentality to *underestimate* poor treatment. Even if victims do exaggerate current abuses, it comes from their experiences and feelings being discounted and minimized by others and themselves. Exaggerating comes from the need to be heard, but the belief that they don't deserve to be heard.

Day 320

Paying attention to negative voices within me is a powerful healing tool. If I listen, I can discover and confront the lies that are in my belief system. Until then, I have two voices—the one I want to believe and the one I truly to believe. What I really believe dictates my feelings and behaviors, so that voice is the most powerful. Getting to the root removes the lie from my belief system so I'm free to think and behave according to what I want for my life instead of the way I was programmed.

Day 321

When I was first healing, I saw all the "trigger warning" messages on abuse sites and I concluded that being triggered was harmful. That coincided with my belief that pain was life-threatening. The truth is, feeling triggered isn't damaging. Triggers aren't the problem; avoiding pain is.

Day 322

Until I recognized that I had no say, no part, no responsibility and no blame in my abuse, I continued to be victimized. My anger was directed toward myself and to punish myself, I abused myself and accepted abuse from others. Recognizing that I had been a victim was the beginning of putting a stop to my victimization.

Daily Journal

Day 323

In a healthy family, parents assume responsibility for their own and for their child's well-being. Covert (or emotional) incest is where the parent's emotional needs are met through the child. The child is burdened with the job of maintaining Mom's or Dad's emotions, health, money, reputation, job or other responsibilities. As a survivor of emotional incest, I took on the needs of my father while having my own needs neglected. I learned to be responsible for others and not for myself. I constantly monitored my dad's moods so I could "fix" them. The pattern kept me focused on other people and I thought that "fixing" others would eventually mean my needs would be met—just as I hoped for as a child.

Day 324

How did my parents' abuse and neglect-filled childhoods excuse mine? How did their wounds minimize mine? They were victims too, but there weren't any answers in knowing their pasts. Looking for answers in my parents' abuse kept me focused on them, the same way I had been conditioned to do. My life has been all about taking care of their needs and wants. Understanding them was survival, but it was survival in the abusive system. To live outside of the abusive system, I had to shift the focus to me.

Day 325

All the time I survived in the abusive system by minimizing and discounting my abuse, the child within me was waiting and crying out to be validated and seen. As long as I was discounting my abuse, I was discounting the child with me—and therefore, me.

Day 326

As a victim, I was indoctrinated in the rules of the abusive system. I accepted the abusive rules: A good girl doesn't complain. A good girl doesn't object. A good girl doesn't tell. It was considered rebellious to think and act apart from my abusers. When I first "rebelled" against the abusive rules, I felt guilty. My parents brought on more punishment in the form of rejection, which they called, "discipline". They believed it was their God-given right to have my obedience and their God-given right to do what they had to so I would submit. Today, I know I have not only the right to my own freedom, but the responsibility to maintain it. I won't be following any rules that serve the abusive system anytime soon.

Day 327

It was impossible to discern dangerous situations as long as I was minimizing my abuse. I believed that I "made a big deal about nothing" so I always questioned whether a situation was really that bad or if I was exaggerating it. Being truthful to myself about how bad my abuse was allowed me to be honest about current situations. I learned to trust myself instead of discounting myself the way the abuse had done.

Day 328

For a time, I wondered how my father could do such horrible things to his only daughter, his little girl. But he didn't do those things to his daughter; he perpetrated those abuses on an object. He didn't even see me while he was abusing me. His needs and his gratification were all he saw. No wonder he could deny abusing me so convincingly; to him, I wasn't there.

Day 329

It was difficult to believe and accept that my memories could be true so I searched through old photographs for confirmation of some of the details that I remembered. I was able to confirm a lot of what I recalled, but when it comes to my healing, those details don't really matter. I didn't need to know how old I was or which bedroom it was. The most important part of reconstructing my memories was finding the false messages within them. Seeing the truth isn't about the color of the walls; it's about seeing that I'm a valuable person no matter how I was treated.

Day 330

I used to be afraid that success would mean the weight of too much responsibility. As a child, I was burdened with the responsibility of keeping my family functioning—by keeping the secret, by keeping my parents happy, by being good. I never had the choice of taking it off. That was too much weight for a child, but the false responsibility of my childhood isn't the same as valid responsibility now. As an adult, I'm equipped to handle the tasks that belong to me. I also have the choice of how much responsibility to accept. I can grow into new opportunities at a pace I feel comfortable with.

<u>Day 331</u>

When I was a child, I took on the responsibility of keeping everyone happy to avoid more abuse. The pressure threatened to crush me. Now, when I start to feel crushed by responsibility, I ask myself if I'm taking on the responsibility of taking care of other people. Am I trying to "make" people happy? Am I doing things for others that they should be doing for themselves? Do I think that it's still my job to carry everyone else?

Day 332

Making mistakes was dangerous because mistakes drew attention to my badness; I thought perfection would keep me from being noticed, but if I was too good at something, that drew attention too. Being too successful meant I would be exposed as a fraud or as undeserving. When I was too successful, I'd quit. Even if I loved the thing I quit, I'd find something about it that made it intolerable. My rule was "be good enough, but not too good."

Daily Journal

<u>Day 333</u>

Throughout my childhood I felt constant fear, but denial didn't allow me to identify its source. Even if I had been able to admit to myself, "I'm afraid because my parents are completely untrustworthy and they threaten my existence," I couldn't do anything about it. I learned to discount my fear and as an adult, put myself in harm's way. All the while, I assured myself, "It will be okay." Once I realized my response to fear, when I'd hear myself say that it would be okay, I'd stop myself. It shifted from being the comfort to go forward to my being my signal to stop. I learned to discern my safety or well-being apart from my default role as a powerless victim.

Day 334

Some fear inhibits my life and some fear protects it. My powerlessness as a child taught me to discount the fear that was meant to protect my life, but I obeyed the fear that inhibited my life. I passed up opportunities and experiences. I missed out on adventures and replaced adventure's excitement with the thrill of danger. Part of healing has meant that I've learned to discern my fear. Now, fear doesn't mean "stop"; it means, "stop and evaluate."

Daily Journal

Day 335

Now that I've found my voice, it doesn't mean that I share every emotion or opinion I have. Being true to myself doesn't mean that I insist on having things my way. It means that I hear my voice and validate what I have to say. From a healthy place of feeling heard (by me), I can decide what to share with others and what to keep to myself.

Day 336

My parents preached that family was so important but they betrayed their own flesh and blood. Their actions defined "family" as the system that allowed them to rule. My parents expressed through their behavior that their superiority in authority made them superior in value. Family members weren't important; only they were. When my parents claimed that family was important, they meant that it was important to stay together so that they could continue to rule.

Day 337

Being silly is a way for me to prove that the child within me didn't die and that she is stronger than the abuse. I've noticed that the more I've healed, the longer I let my inner child express herself. I can play for longer periods without the fear of losing control. I used to think that work and structure kept my world from falling apart, but play always told me the truth.

Day 338

As a kid, I held the responsibility to maintain the status quo. I absorbed the pain so my family could go on in the same manner it always had. Keeping everything the same meant some measure of security and as painful as it was, I couldn't afford the challenge of learning a different life. As an adult, change felt particularly threatening but healing required change. Seeing where the fear came from helped me to overcome it.

Daily Journal

<u>Day 339</u>

My healing process has allowed me to become friends with my body. There are some parts of my restoration that have come about intentionally, but some fruit is a result of just taking the next step and the next step and the next step. I think of becoming friends with my body as a byproduct of directing my anger toward my abusers instead of myself, developing compassion for my inner child, and getting free from shame. I'm gentle with myself now instead of being a slave driver. I'm more generous with the time I reserve for myself instead of driving myself to exhaustion trying to serve everyone else. I love myself now and that changes how I treat my body.

Day 340

When I was married to my abusive ex-husband, the rules always changed and the bar was always raised. It didn't leave me any time to think or see the truth since I always felt behind and had to race to keep up. I never even questioned that system. The put-downs and my constant failures confirmed to me that I didn't deserve better and that I was incapable of doing anything to help myself. I desperately wanted to please him, as though his validation was air and water and food. The suffocation and starvation only made me more dependent on him. I'm amazed it was even possible to escape, but now I'm so happy to be living in the fresh air and banquet of my own self-validation.

Daily Journal

<u>Day 341</u>

My lack of power made me feel like the whole world was dangerous. There was no escape from the abuse because that's all there was. When I started to heal, I felt the same way. Sometimes, giving myself a break from healing allowed me to see that there is a life outside of sexual abuse and that the whole world isn't divided between victims and abusers. I needed that kind of clarity and hope to keep me going.

Day 342

All my life, I adapted to other people. When I started to heal, I had to distance myself from people who had their own ideas about who I should be or what I should do. I could tell that some people were uncomfortable with my healin-process, especially about my anger, or about exposing my parents' abuse. They tried to fix me or rush me through some of the steps. Sometimes it was overt, but most of the time, they didn't say anything, I just knew they didn't approve. It didn't make me act any differently, but it did drag me down. I was exhausted around them. That became my test for everyone—I had to stay away from people who exhausted me so I could reserve my energy for healing.

Day 343

Talking about abuse may trigger the pain of abuse, but it doesn't cause pain. Abuse causes pain. Being silenced causes pain. Talking it out is the beginning of validating the damage of abuse. That's painful, but it's not harmful.

Day 344

When I started healing, I was particularly sensitive to people who didn't honor my boundaries. I couldn't be around people who didn't respect my no. It was small things like when I told my friend that I needed to get off the phone. I was saying no to more talking. One friend would say, "Okay, let me just tell you one more thing," and it would take ten minutes. I noticed she couldn't hear no in other areas either. If I told her I couldn't help her with something, she'd say something like, "I guess I'll have to find someone who loves me." She'd say it in a joking way, but it was a way to manipulate me into saying yes. I wasn't very good at expressing my boundaries yet, but since I was already in so much pain over my sexual, physical, emotional, and mental boundaries being violated, I could afford to add more pain to it. Saying no to a friendship with her meant saying yes to me. I was validating my rights and value even if she wasn't.

Day 345

I started really getting good at protecting myself from certain situations when I started recognizing my inner child. She's the one who was so wounded and filled with fear. I started paying attention to the things she was afraid of and stopped trying to force her into bad situations that would just add to the pain. If I were protecting a child, I could say no. Now, I'm able to say no for the adult me and that feels really good.

Day 346

As painful as it was to face, being ostracized by my parents was an improvement over having them in my life. As bad as it was, I loved myself through it. I couldn't have said the same if I'd have stayed in a relationship with them. To have been accepted by them meant rejecting myself.

Daily Journal

<u>Day 347</u>

With sexual abuse, there's no emotional intimacy. There is no relationship—only a perpetrator and an object. In my sexual relationships, I continued to separate sex from emotional intimacy, since that's the way I learned it.

Day 348

My boundary issues with other people were really boundary issues with myself. I didn't know where I began and ended, but when I reestablished "me" through my healing, the other issues resolved.

Daily Journal

Day 349

When I started to believe that I was worthy of being loved and that I was just as worthy and valuable as everyone else, I started to treat myself with love. The way I started taking care of myself gave a message to those around me that I expected to be treated with value. As I changed my relationship with myself, my other relationships changed too.

Day 350

On my healing journey from childhood sexual abuse—and all the other abuses that accompanied it—I've discovered so many of the so-called keys to healing actually prevented me from healing. My childhood was already so filled with lies that I was desperate for the truth. Though the truth is very often painful, it's also been the only thing that has healed me. Lies kept me imprisoned to the effects of abuse, but the truth sets me free. I've learned to question everything, especially the "truths" that "everyone" knows and distributes so freely. I started to wonder, if they are so true and so many people know about them, then why is the world so screwed up? So my truth test is to look at the fruit of those truths. What actions do those beliefs produce? Do they end in freedom or bondage? What do those "truths" really mean?

Day 351

In the transition of owning my power, I was controlling and heavy-handed. Even though I was starting to own my voice, I was still full of fear. Out of my fear, I sometimes reacted too harshly. Eager to defend my position, I jumped to conclusions about people's motives and came on too strong. I found that my fear and insecurity were amplifying the threat or perceived threat. I thought I was matching intensity, but I was escalating. Once I dealt with the fear (actually, it was over a long period of time even though I changed my behavior immediately), I stopped reacting. I was able to evaluate each situation in a more healthy way. Now, I'm secure with my personal power. I don't feel the need to exert power over anyone else, even those who try to exert power over me. Having power over me is enough.

Day 352

When I was in my crisis period of healing, I had a hard time not accusing myself of being weak. It was difficult to handle the normal responsibilities that an adult should be able to handle. I had the sense that I was a burden and unlovable. Not being able to perform turned out to be very good for me because I had to challenge my belief that I was only good for what I could do for others.

Day 353

For most of my life, I saw my parents the way I wanted and needed to see them. Out of my desperation to see my needs met, I refused to release them from the role I needed them to fill. I continued to see them as loving and caring people even with evidence throughout my adult years that should have shown me the truth. Slowly, as I learned to take care of my own needs, I let go of the fantasy and released them from the role they were unwilling to fulfill.

Day 354

If you are trading silence or compliance for love, you are being cheated. When acceptance or love is withheld if you reveal secrets, the value of the relationship is just an illusion. Love cannot be earned, bought or traded—only freely given. You are worthy of love that doesn't require you to protect your abuser or sacrifice yourself.

Daily Journal

Day 355

After being involved with two legal cases related to abuse, I know that emotional issues can't be resolved in the court system. Both cases turned out favorably but there's no real satisfaction from that. There is no justice after abuse. There is nothing that a judge can do to restore what was lost. There is no punishment for the abuser that can mend the wounds. There is nothing that equals a lost childhood so "waiting for what's fair" means waiting forever. Though I didn't find resolution with the courts, I did find it within myself.

Day 356

The truth is that my value doesn't come from anyone else and it does not go up or down based on what I do. I am valuable because I exist.

Day 357

I blamed myself for being vulnerable. Vulnerability felt like a banner that announced, "Come and get me!" But when I think of it the other way, I don't pounce on other people just because I can. I don't go around looking for people smaller or weaker than me so I can attack them. When I find someone's vulnerability, my impulse is to protect and cover them, not to use it against them.

Day 358

As I'm doing memory work, I stay conscious of what I'm feeling. Having the urge to jump up and do something else, or to escape in some other way, is an indication that I need to slow down and comfort myself. Staying present and allowing the pain to surface is one of the most compassionate things I can do for myself. It's a message to myself that I'm worthy of love and that I don't deserve to be abandoned.

Day 359

All my life, I'd judged my body the way my dad and others did. If I saw something about my body that was considered a flaw to others, especially men, I considered it a flaw too. In victim mentality, pleasing others was the way I survived so anything about me that wasn't "pleasing" was my enemy. Through my harsh treatment and neglect, I'd turned on my body just as violently as my abusers had.

Day 360

Contrary to what I learned in the abusive system, emotions are wonderful. Being disconnected from my emotions meant I was disconnected from my experiences, my self and my entire life. Embracing all of my emotions, in fact, embracing the fact that I am an emotional being, has helped me feel whole, as though my life is mine. Accepting my emotions is accepting me. Emotions are a gift that connects me, not only to myself, but to others. Emotions communicate things that are impossible to comprehend in any other way. I rejected my feelings to survive in the abusive system, but I had to embrace them to really live.

Daily Journal

<u>Day 361</u>

When I first started to remember specific memories of abuse, I felt like I had a storm cloud over me for about two or three days beforehand. When the memory finally surfaced, I felt like I was alone in a dark cave. I stayed in bed just thinking and crying and eating chocolate. I wrote in my healing journal and talked it out with a friend. I examined what I thought and how I felt and cried some more. It was agonizing. The more issues I faced, the stronger I got. It wasn't a pleasant process, but I knew it would be over in a few days and I would feel alive again. With each memory, I recovered faster and I had longer and longer breaks in between them. Facing them made me stronger. I was able to see more and more of the truth without it overwhelming me. Even though the memories increased in intensity, it was easier to deal with them.

Day 362

Self-care is a process. It's one of the biggest challenges of the healing process but it's also one of the biggest rewards. When you can take care of yourself, when you are the priority in your life, when you love yourself, when you don't consider yourself a burden, when you can truly love yourself, everything else falls into place. I consider that wholeness. That is what overcoming is all about.

Day 363

Part of my healing has been the transition of being directed by others to being directed by me. I hear and respect my voice above anyone else's. I'm not limited by what everyone else thinks; I'm more concerned about what I think. The healing process has revealed my own inner wisdom and I've learned to trust in the answers I have for my own life. I'm open to wise counsel from people I trust, but I have the most trust in myself.

Day 364

When I look back at my years of healing from my abuse, I've faced a lot of pain but I've also experienced a lot of pride—for surviving and for healing. I used to be covered in shame and wished to be invisible; now I celebrate who I am and what I've accomplished. I don't wait for other people to acknowledge my successes; I'm the first to share them. I used to be my biggest critic; now I'm my biggest cheerleader. Yay me!

<u>Day 365</u>

I don't know what I would have been like if I hadn't been abused. I don't know what kind of choices I would have made or how my life would have been different. I can't change any of that, but I can change the course of my life now. Abuse set me on a path of self-destruction, but my healing has set me on a new course of self-love and self-validation. I'm making decisions that are joy-filled and life-affirming. Abuse doesn't get the last word; I do.

For more articles and additional support for male
and female survivors of sexual abuse, I invited you
to join us at: www.overcomingsexualabuse.com

Made in the USA
San Bernardino, CA
20 December 2014